D0014234

CONVIVIAL POLICIES FOR THE INEVITABLE

By the same author:

School Science for Tomorrow's Citizens, Pergamon, Oxford 1963

Science and Society: the meaning of scientific method, University of London Press, 1968

European Environment 1975-2000, Conservation Trust, Reading 1972

Practical Classroom Organisation in the Primary School, Ward Lock, London 1978

Nine Hundred Primary School Teachers, NFER Publishing Co, Slough 1978

Teaching Practice in the Primary School, Ward Lock, London 1989

Creating Education through Research, Kirklington Moor Press 1992

Case Study Research in Educational Settings, Open University Press, Buckingham 1999

Teachers and Government: a History of Intervention in Education, ATL, London 2005

Education for the Inevitable: Schooling When the Oil Runs Out, Book Guild Publishing 2011

CONVIVIAL POLICIES FOR THE INEVITABLE

Global Warming, Peak Oil, Economic Chaos

Michael Bassey

Book Guild Publishing
Sussex, England

Dedicated to the generation of my grandchildren,
Sarah, Laura and Oscar.

First published in Great Britain in 2012 by
The Book Guild Ltd
Pavilion View
19 New Road
Brighton, BN1 1UF

Typesetting in Garamond by
YHT Ltd, London

Printed and bound in Great Britain by
CPI Antony Rowe

A catalogue record for this book is available from
The British Library.

ISBN 978 1 84624 806 1

Contents

Part Three: Rethinking for the Inevitable

Preface

In the preface to my *Education for the Inevitable: Schooling When the Oil Runs Out* (2011), I explained why I had written with these words: 'When a retired academic like me, who doesn't play golf or bowls but reads the *Guardian* every weekday and the *Observer* on Sunday, broods on macro-politics and ecology and thinks of his grandchildren and their generation, then it becomes imperative to try to persuade others that urgent actions are needed.' In that book I argue that resolving some of the problems of education requires action outside schools as much as inside them and includes issues such as economic growth, oil peaking and global warming, as well as the role of the press as an educator of adults. The present book explores these economic and ecological issues and others in greater depth.

The summary that follows shows that I have related a wide range of social issues to the problems of global warming, peak oil and economic chaos. When they are set in the ethical framework of conviviality, I believe there is a fundamental coherence to the ideas put forward. For those who are new to the notion of conviviality, it is a way of living through which people gain quality of life and enjoy happiness by striving to be in harmony with themselves and with their social, cultural and natural environments. For each individual this can be a lifelong learning project; for every society it can be the source of peace, prosperity and sustainability. It is the antithesis of wealth creation.

I realise that many may see this not so much as 'Convivial Policies for the Inevitable' as 'Convivial Policies that are Impractical'. They will mutter that politics is the art of the possible and that, while academics can muse about ideal worlds, politicians have to act in the real world. Of course. But the real world is changing fast and reliable predictions indicate that adverse climate change and resource depletion are accelerating and will greatly exacerbate the current chaos in the economic systems of the so-called developed world. Anyone who reflects seriously on this will see that we desperately need politicians who grasp these uncomfortable facts, and who have the courage to tell the nation how it is and the energy and insight to search for ways of achieving a sustainable future.

A Summary of the Key Ideas

1. Recognise that the end of economic growth in the developed countries of the world is an integral part of saving the planet from global warming.
2. Likewise, recognise that while peak oil (this term refers to the point at which demand exceeds production, as the oil wells dry up, and the price soars) may be disastrous for our affluent way of life, it will also be an integral part of saving the planet from global warming by reducing the outpouring of greenhouse gases into the atmosphere; hence eschew extracting oil from tar sands or from the Arctic waters.
3. Don't try to rebuild the old economic system – create a new one of stability, sustainability, and succour for the poor of the world based on a convivial ethos instead of wealth creation. Conviviality is taken to mean living in harmony with one's natural, cultural and social environments and with one's inner self, and recognising these as the roots of human joy, social justice and ecological sanity. We are now the richest generation that has ever lived on this planet – let us act wisely to safeguard the quality of life of our grandchildren and of theirs.
4. Re-orientate the UK economy by introducing a fair minimum living wage and a maximum take-home pay and by replacing the complexities of most benefit and tax credit systems with a universal citizen's income (financed by the

state from taxation) which gives minimal support to the out-of-work and those who can't engage in paid work – like children, students, voluntary workers, the elderly, the infirm, and those who support family members at home.

5. Recognise that unemployment is an incurable phenomenon and, since worthwhile activity is an essential part of joyful life, re-orientate our society so that unpaid work at home or community (supported by citizen's income) is recognised for its intrinsic value.
6. Recognise that, as oil prices soar, personal and freight transport will be severely curtailed, and so develop the idea of partly self-sustaining communities where those without paid jobs find worthwhile activity in home care, allotments and other unpaid work. Organise this on the basis of parishes with mayors, subdivided into manors with reeves.
7. Recognise that we must drastically reduce our energy consumption. But nuclear energy is not the answer – unless a solution to radioactive wastes can be found that does not imperil future generations. We must accelerate the construction of off-shore and onshore wind turbines, begin to re-orient our industries to creating the means of self-sufficiency, plant extensive plots of fast-growing trees for wood burners, ensure that every building where people live or work is thoroughly insulated against the cold of winter, invest heavily in domestic solar panels for hot water and for electricity, and work intelligently in all the directions suggested by ideas of self-sustainability, including massive research and development projects on electrical storage and hydrogen usage. At a personal level, there is one step that it is easy to take: get sufficient warm clothes and buy a bicycle!
8. Recognise that with oil peaking, we will need to change some of the sources of our food and its distribution, and to some extent our diet. The UK will need to become nearly self-

sufficient. Farmers will need to return to organic manures and crop rotation. Local production to avoid long-distance freight will be necessary. Allotments and vegetable gardens should thrive. We will need to eat less meat and enjoy foods in season.

9. Rethink how people obtain money. From paid work, yes; from investment. yes; from speculative gambling, no. We must ask: what is the social value of the frenetic buying and selling of shares in the world markets? The slave trade was once seen as a legitimate way to make fortunes, so was child labour. Both were gross abuses of other human beings. Perhaps stock exchanges should be seen in the same light. Bubbles burst. One person's profit is another's loss.
10. Rethink democracy. It is our most precious asset – our defence against the autocrats and would-be tyrants who try to run public affairs. There are four fundamental principles: the rule of law, the rule of majority, the rule of freedom and the rule of social justice. These enable the entitlement to a good quality of life to be defined. Freedom of the press is an essential part of this. It must be the freedom to inform people of what is happening in our society and the freedom to debate serious issues, but with a freedom from excessive bias (either right wing, as with most of the press today, or left wing) and a freedom from the political predilections of its owners. It must become an agent of adult education in order to debate fairly ideas such as those put forward here.
11. Rethink education. Recognise that the current school curriculum is geared to the failing world of today: business as usual; financial whizz-kids wanted; entrepreneurs needed to boost exports; obedient factory workers and clerical workers with high literacy and computer skills required; the focus on an ethos of competition, a me-first culture and a society ruled by a feral elite. Instead, for their survival, young people need to develop physical fitness, cognitive skills, social

sensitivities, civic skills and environmental understanding. For their quality of life they deserve convivial values and cultural knowledge in many branches. As citizens they need empowerment to achieve a collaborative and sustainable way of life based on critical reflection about society. These are matters of lifelong learning which must begin firmly at school and be experienced joyfully. Too little of this is happening in our schools today. We need community schools where educational decisions are made by teachers working collegially, supported by local governors, and financed but not controlled by central government.

12. There can be little doubt that there are tough times ahead. Austerity inevitably defines the agenda. There will be those who say that these are 'kill-joy' measures that will deprive people of their pleasures: self-fulfilling shopping therapy, air flights to distant lands, proud display of better vehicles than the neighbours', over-mortgaged homes, choice of expensive private schools, expenditure on private health care and cosmetic surgery, delight in designer-modelled clothes, state-of-the art music systems, electronic gadgets, visits to expensive restaurants, little-used boats in a distant marina, and so on. Yes, in a more equal society without economic growth, these pleasures will disappear. But these are extrinsic pleasures which can give way to simpler, cheaper and possibly more enduring intrinsic pleasures derived from working and living in local communities, enjoying cultural and sporting pursuits and finding joy in simple things.

Fundamentally I am an optimist. I believe people can establish a stable, sustainable and worthwhile quality of life for themselves and for future generations. But to achieve this, every adult, every child, has to work hard at it in order to learn how to replace the greed of wealthism and a me-first culture with the joy of conviviality and by sharing in community life.

Introduction

Why didn't anyone see it coming?

—HM Queen Elizabeth II (2008)

Two Tales from a Nottinghamshire Village

In 1846 the railway line between Nottingham and Newark, in the East Midlands of England, was built, with stations at each of the villages in between. In Burton Joyce the railway company had wanted a station near to the centre of the village by one of the pubs, the Lord Nelson, but the landlord objected. His argument was that if the station was near to his pub he would have to brew more beer and he was not prepared to do this. He prevailed and the station was built half a mile further down the line. We can imagine that he had sufficient income from the existing trade for him and his family to have a quiet, comfortable life. He did not want to work harder, or employ more labour, in order to increase his profits. He had enough: he was content.[1]

More recently, when I lived in the same village (much enlarged since Victorian times), one evening I was having a beer in another of the local pubs with a friend who managed a small factory for the Bell Fruit Company. Maybe it was an alcoholic haze that induced me to put a personal question to him. I asked, 'How is it that, with your concerns for people and managerial skills, you're wasting your life on making gambling machines?' He answered promptly, 'No Mike, you don't understand. What I am actually doing is enabling the hundred or so people in my factory to take home every week a wage packet that provides food, housing and the other necessities of life for them and their families. They trust me to manage well and I trust them to work well.'

Business Must Grow or Die?

What a contrast between the values of these two men and the prevailing ethos of the business world. The success of a business is too often judged by whether it has made more money this year than last. When Sir Terry Leahy, boss of Tesco, retired in 2011, he said:

> In every business the chief executive wakes up in the morning wondering where the growth will come from.[2]

If big business has to make redundant some of its workforce in order to achieve a profit, so be it – that is the bosses' view. 'That's the way of the world. It's progress. Grow or die.'

It must be said that this is more the ethos of many of the big companies, less so that of the smaller businesses. Family grocers and butchers in the high street, for example, are usually content if their takings year by year are steady. But they are being eroded by the competition of supermarkets striving to grow bigger. Likewise, one-person businesses such as plumbers, electricians and house decorators are usually content with a steady flow of work, while the bigger enterprises in these fields seek to expand their trade.

The End of Economic Growth

Economic growth is not a universal good. In terms of the contemporary understanding by scientists of man-made global warming, the above motto 'Grow or die' is better expressed as 'Grow *and* die'. We must begin to see economic growth in a rich country like ours as a globally destructive force contributing devastatingly to climate change, oil peaking, droughts, food shortages, loss of fisheries, sea-level change, and the possibility of resource wars and civil unrest that may result from these. In poorer countries, on the other hand, economic growth is needed in order to raise the quality of life – but such countries should look for sustainable ways forward and not aspire to the disastrous ends that we have sought. Economies across the world should aim to converge at some time in the future at levels of need, not greed, which give everyone a reasonable quality of life.

We have to be educated about growth. In the human body as in society, growth is needed to turn infancy into adolescence into adulthood; thereafter, growth is a cancer which sooner or later destroys the body.

Economic growth needs to give way to cultural growth. We need to learn how to value and enjoy what we have, how to create without damaging the planet, and how to live convivially.

One of my pursuits in retirement is writing letters to the press. I hope they read as from 'Angry old man of Coddington, Nottinghamshire' rather than from the proverbial 'Disgusted of Tunbridge Wells'. On a recent count I get about one in six published. Looking back through the file I see that they represent the development in recent years of my political understanding and, indeed, are part of the backcloth to this book. Hence, where appropriate, I shall slip some of them into this text.

Early in 2010 Gordon Brown, Prime Minister, was talking about the need to create a 'class-free society' and a 'genuine meritocracy'. I took issue with him, as this letter in the *Guardian* of 19 January 2010 shows:

> In 1945, the Attlee government took heed of the Beveridge report calling for the abolition of the 'five giants' of that time – want, ignorance, disease, squalor, and idleness. Would that Brown's government would respond to the five giants of today – inequality, greed, self-interest, unemployment and indifference. Would that he talked of quality of life and happiness of people rather than the obsession with climbing a social ladder of affluence. Economic growth is not the answer for a developed country like the UK. What is needed is ecological sustainability. This will require more equality, protection for the unemployed, community strength, mutual support and greater self-sufficiency in food and energy production. That is the agenda he should be offering the electorate and one which would move us towards a classless society in which meritocracy could safely thrive.

By July 2011 the British economy had been static for almost a year. When it is too painful for economists to admit that the economy has stopped growing, they use the euphemism 'flatlined'. A report in the *Guardian* that the government was struggling to explain why this is happening prompted me to send the following letter to the editor which, to my surprise, was published (28 July 2011), with the heading spread across the page:

> **The End of Economic Growth**
>
> Noting that the economy 'has flatlined for almost a year' you report that 'Cameron sets up defences ahead of storm over [lack of] growth' (26 July). Instead of fighting it, isn't it time that government, opposition, and trade unions began to plan how to flatline with social justice?
>
> An end to economic growth? Yes, inevitable. In June 2000 the Labour government set up a Sustainable Development Commission. In 2009 Professor Tim Jackson, a senior member of this SDC,

produced the report *Prosperity without Growth*. He wrote: '*Every society clings to a myth by which it lives. Ours is the myth of economic growth. ... It's totally at odds with our scientific knowledge of the finite resource base and the fragile ecology on which we all depend for survival.*' The SDC was closed by the government in March.

There are plenty of ideas around on how to flatline: a citizen's income to protect those without work; a take-home-pay differential of one to 10 (severe taxation of the opulent) to cut the deficit; a four-day week for most workers to share around the available work; community development to protect the vulnerable, aged and infirm; a massive development of allotments to move towards self-sufficiency in food; energy reduction policies like 'the more you use the greater the unit charge' to move towards self-sufficiency in energy; and all this supported by adult education via the media that explains the dire predicament of 'a finite resource base' and 'fragile ecology'.

These measures would disrupt the lives of most of us, especially the well-to-do, but they would prepare us for the grave uncertainties of the near future – and give meaning to the prime minister's claim that 'we are all in this together'.

Most business people, politicians and economists reject the idea that we should no longer look for economic growth. Those few who recognise the validity of the case for zero growth say, 'Not yet.' Like St Augustine, they pray, 'Oh Lord, make me chaste, but not yet.' Today is too near, they say. Too near? Perhaps. But the earth is heating up year by year and oil is about to peak, as discussed in two later chapters.

A Green No-Growth Revolution

The United Kingdom pioneered the Industrial Revolution: can it now pioneer a green no-growth revolution? The country which started the economic restructuring of society with the Industrial Revolution could now seek and try out radical ways of *ecologically* structuring society with a green revolution. Fundamentally, unless we in the West start to consume less – by buying fewer goods, by putting less heat into our homes, by transporting goods less, by cutting our travel on ground and air so that we guzzle less oil – carbon dioxide levels in the atmosphere will continue to rise, the global climate will continue to deteriorate, oil reserves will run out more quickly, and the lives of our descendants will be blighted by our greed and folly.

Naturally, the aspirations of developing countries are for the same levels of affluence as the West has at present, and so the world future is bleak. We can only expect fast-growing economies like China, India and Brazil to seek a different path to progress for their peoples if we in the over-developed economies start to cut back.

The current global challenge needs a massive mind-shift worldwide. It is not a recession that we should fear, but the dearth of statesmen who have the insight and courage to develop an ecological economy which protects both the people and the environment.

What this amounts to is a fundamental re-think of our current way of life: a green-no-growth revolution underpinned by an ethos of conviviality. This is what this book is about.

Entitlements for All

From time to time, everyone interested in politics should ask: 'What do I think are the entitlements of children and adults in this country today?' To strive for these entitlements should be the *raison d'être* of every politician. The question is, of course, part of a bigger question which human beings, alone among the animal kingdom, can ask – namely: 'What is my life about?'

After due cogitation, this list constitutes my answer at the moment – that is, until someone points out things I've left out which I would want in, or until I register them myself.

For the adult:

- Work opportunities that provide sufficient income for needs, and that are personally satisfying and not over-demanding of personal time;
- A comfortable home for self and any family;
- Good opportunities to obtain food and other essentials of domestic life;
- Social opportunities that enable one to relate to others and build friendships;
- Leisure and entertainment opportunities and time to enjoy them;
- Travel opportunities;
- Freedom from fear, and enjoyment of peace and tranquillity;
- Democratic freedoms, including living under the rule of law and benefiting from electoral opportunities;
- Medical provision in sickness and in health, and good care in old age;
- Lifelong learning opportunities.

And if some of these are missing, or in short supply:

- Hope that things will soon improve.

For the child:

- Safe nurturing by loving adults who share with the child, as appropriate, the other entitlements listed above;
- Education in good schools;
- Happy friendships;
- Good opportunities for play.

Having drawn up this list, I am much aware that I have had a fortunate life in having had these entitlements manifest, but many people in today's world, in Britain, but more so in some other parts of the world, do not.

There are people who have no work. There are people who live in inadequate housing, who may be hungry, cold, impoverished and have given up hope of anything better. There are people who live in fear – of the neighbours, of losing their housing, of lacking care in old age. There are people for whom there is no community – just strangers in the same street.

In Britain today there are people who have been jobless for years, living in poverty with their families, fearful that the government may cut their benefits, and lacking utterly in hope that things will improve.

In November 2011, over 8% of the potential workforce of the UK was unemployed. But we are not alone. Statistics from the European Commission[3] show that all of our neighbours have serious levels of unemployment: Spain, 23%; Greece, 19%; Ireland, 15%; Portugal, 13.5%; Poland, 10%; France, 10%; Italy, 9%; Denmark, 8%; Sweden, 7%; Belgium, 7%; Finland, 7%; Germany, 5.5%; the Netherlands, 5%. Joblessness is endemic in the industrial (supposedly rich) countries. In the United States in November 2011 unemployment was 8.5%.[4]

Worse, in some of the poorer countries of the world, where there are people who are jobless, living in extreme poverty, and fearful of brutality and mercilessness from those in authority, there is the currently developing fear of famine, drought and dangerous weather conditions brought on by global warming.

So, these entitlements are starting points for exploring some political ideas.

Horsemen of the Apocalypse

In popular culture, the four horsemen of the apocalypse were War, Death, Famine and Pestilence. Today we can hear the hooves of three of the current harbingers of doom: Global Warming, Peak Oil and Economic Chaos. Let us hope there is not a fourth one – which could be Nuclear War, Uncontrollable Plague, Widespread Infertility, Volcanic Blackout, or a peril as yet unrecognised. The three that we can hear (if we listen) are discussed in Part One.

The ethos of conviviality is discussed in Part Two as a viable alternative to the endless pursuit of wealth, and Part Three suggests ideas for forward-looking politicians. These ideas concern rethinking the following: income and taxation (Chapter 6); work and communities (Chapter 7); energy supplies (Chapter 8); food supplies (Chapter 9); money and investment (Chapter 10); democracy and the role of the media (Chapter 11); and education for future survival (Chapter 12). No doubt many of the protesters on the steps of St Paul's Cathedral, who called themselves 'the 99%', will find agreement with at least some of these ideas.

Finally, the Endpoint returns to the theme of entitlements of a citizen and suggests that, even in the coming time of severe austerity, the propositions put forward in this book would provide hope that these entitlements could become reality for everybody.

Part One: The Inevitable

1

The Inevitable: An End to Economic Growth

> *In the human body as in society, growth is needed to turn infancy into adolescence into adulthood: thereafter growth is a cancer which sooner or later destroys the body.*
>
> M.B.

Inevitable Decline of Industrial Societies

In 1972 two books were published on a perceived end to economic growth: *A Blueprint for Survival*,[5] by a group of English conservationists, and *The Limits to Growth*,[6] by the Club of Rome. The first stated bluntly that 'the principal defect of the industrial way of life with its ethos of expansion is that it is not sustainable'. This view was based on the common sense ruminations of its authors. The second book predicted that 'the most probable result [of current growth trends] will be a sudden and uncontrollable decline in both population and industrial capacity'. It was based on computer-based analyses of complex world systems and, because critics could come to grips with the reasoning, was widely challenged.

There was a tendency for scientists to support the doom-laden predictions without much challenge, for economists to oppose them because they threatened their holy cow of economic growth, for industrialists to scorn them because they attacked their *raison d'être*, and for politicians to treat them as a seven-day wonder and then forget them.

I was one who accepted the central idea of *Blueprint* as self-evident. It was the basis for Figure 1, a chart which I drew for a Conservation Trust campaign in 1973. Still being of the same mind in 1987, I reproduced it in my professorial inaugural lecture at Trent Polytechnic in that year.

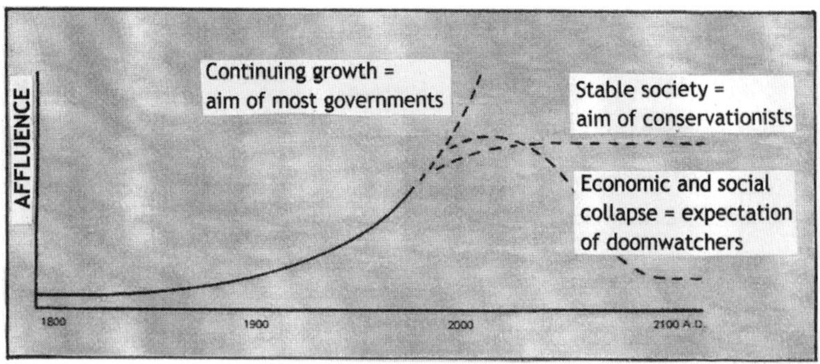

Figure 1. Levels of Affluence in the UK from 1800 AD to 2100 AD

In recent years, few people talking of the future seem to recognise the inevitability of industrial decline and the urgent need to find fulfilling and worthwhile jobs away from the factories and offices where so many people work today. Moreover, few see that economic growth must at some time come to an end.

Young Fabians Look Fifty Years Ahead (But Wearing Blinkers!)

For example, a booklet published in October 2010 by the Young Fabians, entitled *The New Generation: participating in change for the next 50 years*, certainly recognises that there are major problems ahead:

> Climate change will damage the industries and livelihoods that power economics. However, with economic failure comes an opportunity – the opportunity to reshape the foundations of economies so that they can grow in a green and sustainable way. What has been termed as the 'Hydra-headed crisis' – the series of interdependent, systemic challenges (energy and food security, jobless growth, climate change, global governance) facing countries, institutions and individuals alike – requires a holistic approach and decisive action.

This passage comes from a chapter by Adam Short which goes on to refer to a 'green recovery' and discusses issues such as energy security; house insulation; smart meters; and changing planning regulations to allow wood to be used in construction, house owners to generate energy, and local communities to build wind farms. But he sees these in terms of *economic growth*, mentioned eleven times in nine pages, and usually described as *green and equitable growth.*

How has he missed (or rejected) the 132-page report of the Sustainable Development Commission (SDC)?

Prosperity without Growth? *A report of the SDC,* dated March 2009

The Sustainable Development Commission was a non-departmental public body responsible for advising the government on sustainable development. It was set up by the Labour Government in June 2000. Professor Tim Jackson, Economic Commissioner of the SDC, wrote in the foreword to *Prosperity Without Growth*:[7]

> Every society clings to a myth by which it lives. Ours is the myth of economic growth. . . . It's totally at odds with our scientific knowledge of the finite resource base and the fragile ecology on which we depend for survival. . . .
>
> The default assumption is that – financial crises aside – growth will continue indefinitely. Not just for the poorest countries, where a better quality of life is undeniably needed, but even for the richest

nations where the cornucopia of material wealth adds little to happiness and is beginning to threaten the foundations of our wellbeing.

The reasons for this collective blindness are easy enough to find. The modern economy is structurally reliant on economic growth for its stability. When growth falters – as it has done recently – politicians panic. Businesses struggle to survive. People lose their jobs and sometimes their homes. A spiral of recession looms. Questioning growth is deemed to be the act of lunatics, idealists and revolutionaries.

But question it we must. The myth of growth has failed us. It has failed the two billion people who still live on less that $2 a day. It has failed the fragile ecological systems on which we depend for survival. It has failed, spectacularly, in its own terms, to provide economic stability and secure people's livelihoods.

Today we find ourselves faced with the imminent end of the era of cheap oil, the prospect (beyond the recent bubble) of steadily rising commodity prices, the degradation of forests, lakes and soils, conflicts over land use, water quality, fishing rights and the momentous challenge of stabilising concentrations of carbon in the global atmosphere. And we face these tasks with an economy that is fundamentally broke, in desperate need of renewal.

In these circumstances, a return to business as usual is not an option. . . .

Prosperity consists in our ability to flourish as human beings – within the ecological limits of a finite planet. The challenge for our society is to create the conditions under which this is possible. It is the most urgent task of our times.

Prosperity without Growth argues that growth is driven by the dynamic of production and consumption of novelty and that somehow this needs to end. It argues for heavy investment targeted carefully at energy security, low-carbon infrastructures and ecological protection, and work-time policies that result in people spending more time in leisure, giving more opportunity for otherwise unemployed people to work. In all, it puts forward twelve steps towards creating a sustainable economy.

The SDC was closed down by the coalition government in

March 2011 – an act of ideology and nihilism which surely verges on lunacy, particularly when, at the time of writing, the economy of Britain has stopped growing. This used to be called 'stagnating', but recently the less emotive term 'flatlining' has been used. Perhaps this is the beginning of acceptance by the economic establishment that we are approaching the end of economic growth.

Scientists Who Worry about Economic Growth

If one searches, there are others who recognise that fundamental change in our economic thinking is needed. The following are edited summaries of three papers from prestigious scientific journals that are examples of such a change in thinking.

(1) **'Overcoming Systemic Roadblocks to Sustainability: the evolutionary redesign of worldviews, institutions and technologies'**, N. Myers and 12 colleagues, *Proceedings of the National Academy of Sciences of the USA* (2009).[8]

Summary: A high and sustainable quality of life is a central goal for humanity. The lifestyles of the industrial countries of the world all support the goal of unlimited growth of material production and consumption as a proxy for quality of life. However, abundant evidence shows that, beyond a certain threshold, further material growth no longer significantly contributes to improvement in quality of life. Not only does further material growth not meet humanity's central goal, there is mounting evidence that it creates significant roadblocks to sustainability through increasing constraints (i.e. peak oil, water limitations, and climate disruption). Overcoming these roadblocks in order to try to create a sustainable and desirable future will require a redesign of our lifestyles focused explicitly and directly on the goal of sustainable quality of life rather than on the proxy of unlimited material growth.

In layman's language, the present road to the good life, based on economic growth, is blocked.

(2) **'Shrink and Share: humanity's present and future ecological footprint'**, J. Kitzes and 6 colleagues, *Philosophical Transactions of the Royal Society of London* (2008).[9]

Summary: Sustainability is the possibility of all people living rewarding lives within the means of nature. Despite ample recognition of the importance of achieving sustainable development, exemplified by the Rio Declaration of 1992 and the United Nations Millennium Development Goals, the global economy fails to meet the most fundamental minimum condition for sustainability – that human demand for ecosystem goods and services remains within the biosphere's total capacity. In 2002,

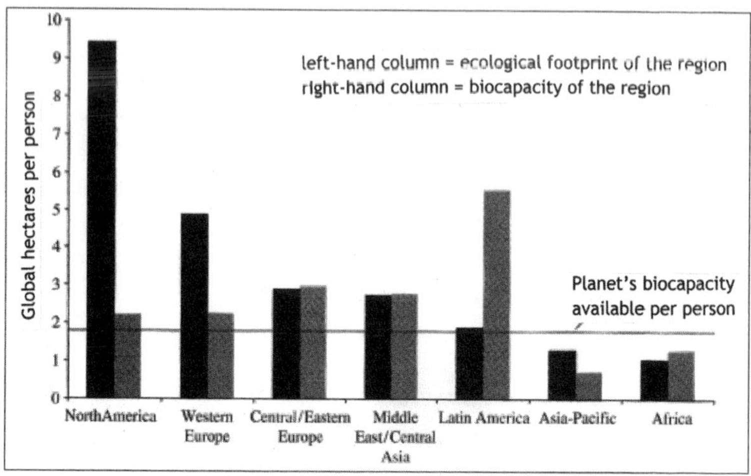

Figure 2. The ecological footprint and biocapacity of different global regions

humanity operated in a state of overshoot, demanding over 20% more biological capacity than the earth's ecosystems could regenerate in that year. Bringing humanity out of overshoot and onto a potentially sustainable path will require managing the consumption of food, fibre and energy, and maintaining or increasing the productivity of natural and agricultural ecosystems.

Figure 2 shows the ecological footprint and biocapacity of different global regions.

In Figure 3, three alternative global paths to the future are identified: (a) the business-as-usual path here is based on projections for carbon emissions and resource demand through to 2050 from the IPCC and FAO; (b) the 'slow-shift' policy-driven path is intended to bring humanity out of overshoot and achieve a level of 90% use of global biological capacity by 2100; (c) the 'rapid reduction' conservation-based path brings humanity out of overshoot before 2050 and stabilises at 70% use of global capacity.

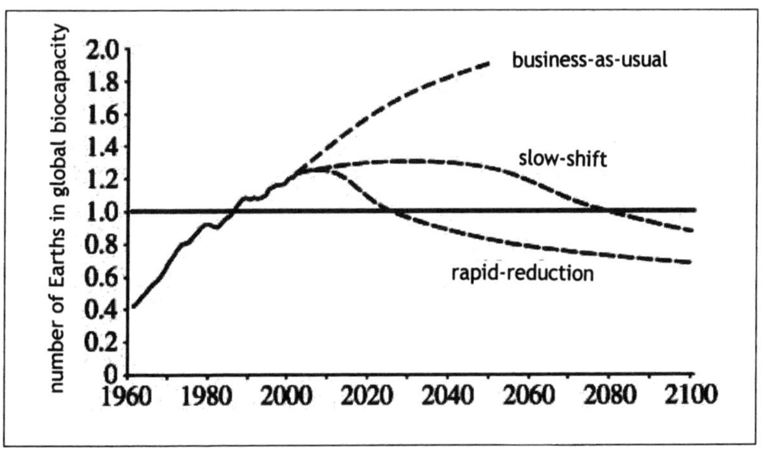

Figure 3. Three Alternative Global Paths to the Future

Paths above the horizontal line show humanity operating in a state of overshoot (i.e. demanding more biological capacity than the earth's ecosystems can produce).

In layman's language, humanity's ecological footprint, in North America, Western Europe and the Asia-Pacific economies, is larger than the earth can sustain. Business as usual in these continents will lead to global Armageddon.

(3) **'Energy Return on Investment, Peak Oil, and the End of Economic Growth'**, D.J. Murphy and C.A. Hall, *Annals of the New York Academy of Science* (2011).

Summary: Economic growth over the past forty years has used increasing quantities of fossil energy, and most importantly, oil. Yet our ability to increase the global supply of conventional crude oil much beyond current levels is doubtful, which may pose a problem for continued economic growth. Our research indicates that, due to the depletion of conventional, and hence cheap, crude oil supplies (i.e. due to peak oil), increasing the supply of oil in the future would require exploiting lower-quality (i.e. expensive) resources, and thus could occur only at a high price. This situation creates a system of feedbacks that can be aptly described as an economic growth paradox: increasing the oil supply to support economic growth will require high oil prices that will undermine that economic growth. From this, the authors conclude that the economic growth of the past forty years is unlikely to continue in the long term unless there is some remarkable change in how we manage our economy.

In layman's language, as the world's oil supplies decline, economic growth will come to an end.

Economists Who Do Not Worry About Economic Growth

Notwithstanding this scientific testimony, the governments of the 'rich world', members of the Organisation for Economic Co-operation and Development (OECD), still espouse economic growth, albeit with an awareness of the ecological problems and what they see as a green re-direction. The OECD Secretary-General, Angel Gurría, writes in the OECD booklet *Towards Green Growth* of 25 May 2011:

> The world economy is slowly, and unevenly, coming out of the worst crisis most of us have ever known.
>
> While dealing with immediate problems such as high unemployment, inflationary pressures or fiscal deficits, we have to look to the future and devise new ways of ensuring that the growth and progress we have come to take for granted are assured in the years to come.
>
> A return to 'business as usual' would indeed be unwise and ultimately unsustainable, involving risks that could impose human costs and constraints on economic growth and development. It could result in increased water scarcity, resource bottlenecks, air and water pollution, climate change and biodiversity loss which would be irreversible. Strategies to achieve greener growth are needed. . . .
>
> At the OECD Ministerial Council Meeting in June 2009, Ministers acknowledged that green and growth can go hand-in-hand, and asked the OECD to develop a Green Growth Strategy.
>
> Since then, we have been working with a wide range of partners from across government and civil society to provide a framework for how countries can achieve economic growth and development while at the same time combating climate change and preventing costly environmental degradation and the inefficient use of natural resources.

This stance is no surprise, since Article One of the Convention, signed on 14 December 1960 in Paris by representatives of the governments of Austria, Belgium, Canada, Denmark, France, Germany, Greece, Iceland, Ireland, Italy, Luxembourg, the Netherlands, Norway, Portugal, Spain, Sweden, Switzerland,

Turkey, the United Kingdom, and the United States of America, states:

> The aims of the Organisation for Economic Co-operation and Development shall be to promote policies designed:
>
> (a) to achieve the highest sustainable economic growth and employment and a rising standard of living in Member countries, while maintaining financial stability, and thus to contribute to the development of the world economy;
> (b) to contribute to sound economic expansion in Member as well as non-member countries in the process of economic development; and
> (c) to contribute to the expansion of world trade on a multilateral, non-discriminatory basis in accordance with international obligations.

Since then, 14 more countries have joined the OECD and signed the convention: Australia, Chile, Czech Republic, Estonia, Finland, Hungary, Israel, Japan, Korea, Mexico, New Zealand, Poland, Slovak Republic, and Slovenia.

I consider that the words 'sustainable' and 'growth' are mutually incompatible and that it is high time these rich countries sought a stable, and therefore sustainable, economy and eschewed any desire to become richer through economic growth. How should we in Britain do this?

Towards a Green No-Growth Economy

Viable ways forward for the UK economy must tackle: the financial meltdown, recession and the rise of unemployment; peak oil; fossil-fuel-induced global warming and climate change; and the greed and power-lust of the rich and mighty. Some agenda!

First, we must recognise that economic growth is the

adolescent stage before a nation reaches economic maturity. Regrettably, our affluence has brought the acne of over-consumption, with dire effects on the global environment. Unless we in the West consume less – by buying fewer goods, putting less heat into our homes, transporting goods less, cutting our travel on ground and air so that we guzzle less oil – carbon dioxide levels in the atmosphere will continue to rise, the global climate will continue to deteriorate, and the lives of our descendants will be blighted by our greed and folly. And when the aspirations of developing countries seek the same levels of affluence as the West has at present, the world future is bleak. We can only expect fast-growing economies like China, India and Brazil to seek a different path to progress for their peoples if we in the over-developed economies start to cut back. Consuming less means the end of economic growth. Achieving a steady-state economy requires a mind-shift by Treasury civil servants, all of our political parties except the Greens, the commercial/industrial business world, and the whole community. Wow!

Second, we must recognise that a steady-state economy will require major changes in the country's jobs profile. Fewer people will be needed to produce, transport and trade consumer goods, more people will be needed for local production of food and for recasting energy production and usage. More people could be engaged in supporting the disabled, the infirm, and the elderly. Whether there will ever be full paid employment is, I believe, very unlikely. A possible alternative, where everyone is employed, but not all paid, is discussed in Chapter 7.

What is certain is that in the transition there will be many people who will lose their jobs and whose families, homes and livelihood will be at dire risk unless this issue is tackled head on. This is where the long-discussed idea of citizen's income is the answer – a modest income paid to every adult man and woman in the country, from government funds, and seen as a citizen's right

– not a benefit to be means-tested and begrudged (Chapter 6). No doubt levels of taxation would need to rise in an ethic in which the rich support the poor. The citizen's income should be index-linked and so, over time, the present gross disparity between rich and poor would be reduced. The Inland Revenue, pension and benefits systems should be merged so that all monies passing between individual and state go through the same agency.

Third, there should be a greed tax which ensures that no one takes home more than ten times the minimum living wage (Chapter 6). This will cause some of the super rich – captains of industry and lieutenants of finance – to emigrate. Let them go, because they are the proponents of ever-increasing consumption and will never understand that economic growth is part of the developed countries' problem. There are plenty of able people with the talent to lead the necessary institutions of this country without seeking obscene levels of remuneration. Symbolically this will help to propagate the Gandhi ethical message that 'there is enough in the world for each person's need, there is not enough for each one's greed'. Fiscally it will help fund the citizen's income.

Fourth, we must stop the speculators from playing with phantom money. Money is a conundrum. At first, people got money by working with brawn or brain and being paid for what they produced or the service they rendered. People with much money could lend some and, by charging interest, acquire more. Likewise, people who owned more land or houses than they needed could let others have the use of them in exchange for rent. People in trade, such as manufacturing and shop-keeping, often needed more money than they possessed. So they would invite people with spare cash to buy shares in their business on the understanding that when the business was successful a share of the profit would go to those who had invested in it. Then came a further – and in the long term disastrous – way of making money: shares could be traded at a stock exchange on the likely chance of the share price rising so that the shares could be sold at a profit. At first the trading was done relatively slowly, by telephone and hand signals, but as technology advanced, the trading could be almost instantaneous by computers working to algorithms. In 2006, 40% of trading on the London Stock Exchange was done by computers. Vast sums of money moved electronically across the world – making fortunes for some as the market value of shares grew. However, it wasn't solid gold that moved, but soap suds – and in 2008 the bubble burst, but now is slowly growing again. Starting from scratch, would a sane society allow ephemeral money to be created by the buying and selling of shares? What if buyers were required to hold on to shares for at least a few months before selling them? Buying shares would then be a matter of wise investment, not hopeful speculation. Could this be another stage in the necessary reform of global capitalism (Chapter 10)?

There is much more of this kind of thinking needed to resolve energy (Chapter 8) and food-provision problems (Chapter 9) to provide for community development (Chapter 7), to promote the educational function of the media (Chapter 11), and to support those countries where there is extreme poverty, drought and starvation. England started the Industrial Revolution; now it could start the ecological revolution – the green no-growth revolution, first in Europe and North America, and then worldwide. Overall, it requires replacing a culture of individualism and greed with an ethic of social responsibility – which I call 'conviviality' (Chapter 4). Could we do it?

2

The Inevitable: An End to Cheap Oil

My father rode a camel, I drive a car, my son flies an airplane, his son will ride a camel.

—Arab saying, 21st century

Beginnings of the Age of Oil

Oil, in its different forms, has been extracted from the earth at least since the fourth century AD, for there are records of wells being drilled in China and the oil coming to the surface through bamboo pipes. They burned it to evaporate brine. By the eighth century an oil industry was thriving in the Middle East, and it was even distilled for military purposes. Oil that came out of the ground in Baku was being used for heating in the thirteenth century. In the early nineteenth century the petroleum distillate kerosene began to be available to replace whale oil in oil lamps, and other products included machine oils and lubricants needed for the machines of the Industrial Revolution. In 1859 petroleum was first mined in Pennsylvania in the United States. It began to have many uses, and with the development of the internal combustion engine in motor cars, demand escalated and many oil deposits across the world were mined.[10]

From less than a million barrels a day being produced in 1900, by 2009 there were 84 million barrels a day coming out of the ground and being treated worldwide in over 700 refineries. Petroleum was mined, refined, and used in the chemical and plastics industries and for transport by car, lorry, plane and ship as though there were no tomorrow. There were fluctuations in the price per barrel, but production and consumption just went up and up.

Foresight – Or Lack Of It

In the UK in 2008 the Government Office for Science (now part of the Department for Business and Industry) published a Foresight report (of 204 pages) entitled 'Sustainable Management and the Built Environment'. It says:

> The UK is entering a period of energy transition. The main forces driving change are a growing consensus about the scale and importance of climate change, and the need to ensure secure energy supplies for the UK in the face of rising global demand.[11]

The report refers to 'the overarching need to set a decarbonisation agenda'; the reason for this is climate change and the need to cut greenhouse gas emissions. Necessary and essential, of course – but what is surprising is that the idea that supplies of oil might be limited in the future and the price shoot up is not considered. In 204 pages there is only one mention of peak oil – in a glossary of terms at the end:

> Peak Oil. Period at which world oil production will reach its maximum and begin to decline. Individual countries such as the US and the UK have passed their oil production peaks and the world as a whole may do so in around 2020.[12]

There is no mention of this in the report itself, and thus one may wonder why they bothered to define it in the glossary! It seems incredible that a Foresight report could say in its appendix that in 12 years' time oil may peak, and yet offer no comment.

Peak Oil Begins To Be Discussed

Just two years later, in February 2010, a group of five senior industrialists, known as the UK Industry Taskforce on Peak Oil and Energy Security, demolished the calm with 'The Oil Crunch: a wake-up call for the UK economy':

> As we reach maximum oil extraction rates, the era of cheap oil is behind us. We must plan for a world in which oil prices are likely to be both higher and more volatile and where oil price shocks have the potential to destabilise economic, political and social activity. Virtually every sector of our economy is still dependent on oil. This is why it is vital that whichever party forms the next government, they have a coherent set of policies to help the UK adapt. This is especially important for the UK, and other developed economies, which have been so reliant on low-cost oil for decades.... Our transport system, which is central to our economy and social fabric, is largely dependent on fossil fuels and older combustion technologies. There is an extraordinary gap between what a number of think tanks and scientists write about the future of oil and the current policies of governments and businesses.[13]

It took 13 months for the UK government to take note of this report, but in March 2011 Chris Huhne, then Secretary of State for Energy and Climate Change, met members of the Industry Taskforce in a closed-door meeting. Chris Nelder, an independent expert on peak oil, trying to find out what happened at the meeting, learned that some important conclusions were reached – namely:

- Peak oil is either here, or close enough.
- Prices will have to go higher as demand outstrips supply.
- Governments will be forced to intervene to maintain critical levels of oil supply, and limit volatility.
- Rationing measures may be unavoidable.
- Electricifiation of transport must be pursued in order to reduce demand.

- Communities will need to work quickly to reorganise around walking instead of driving, producing food and energy locally instead of importing, and generally try to reduce their need for oil.[14*]

Nelder's added note that the notion that peak oil will mean the end of economic growth apparently fell on deaf ears.

March 2011 also saw the publication of a carefully argued academic report from the College of Engineering and Petroleum at Kuwait University forecasting that world production of petroleum would peak in 2014 at around 79 million barrels per day (mbpd). Also in this month, a paper from David King (former UK chief scientist) and researchers at Oxford University anticipated that demand for oil could outstrip supply by 2014–2015.[15]

In June 2011, a freedom of information request forced the UK government to publish its report entitled 'Prospects for Crude Oil Supply and Demand'.[16] Why publication had been resisted is not clear. It was a call to industry and other experts for evidence on the prospects for future oil supply and demand over the next one to forty years. Two 'key messages' were:

- The majority of respondents believe that total oil production will peak before 2030, and many argue that there will be significant supply-side constraints before 2020.
- The majority of responses anticipate that production will plateau and then decline gradually.

Nobody seemed to deny that the supply of oil will at some stage decline; the disagreements centred on how long we've got before this starts, whether it will be a sharp or a steady decline and whether this will be due to the geology or the economics of

* Nelder reported in *Energy Bulletin*, published by Post Carbon Institute, a non-profit organisation dedicated to helping the world transition away from fossil fuels and build sustainable, resilient communities.

drilling for oil. Yes. It is inevitable that the writing is on the wall for the Age of Fossil Oil.

But Still the Oil Companies Look for More

Arctic Oil

Worryingly, at the time of writing in the summer of 2011, with the partial melting of the Arctic ice cap, some of the big oil companies, like Shell and Exxon, were making plans for oil-well drilling in the hitherto frozen north. Memories abound of the Deepwater Horizon catastrophic blowout and oil spill in the Gulf of Mexico in April 2010, which killed 11 people and led to almost 5 million barrels of oil being spilled into the ocean, taking five months to contain; it is reckoned that it will eventually end up costing billions of dollars in clean-up costs and compensation claims. Ben Ayliffe, a Greenpeace campaigner, said:

> A spill in the Arctic would essentially make dealing with something like Deepwater Horizon look almost straightforward. There are problems with ice encroachment, the remoteness of the Arctic, darkness, extreme weather, deep water, high seas, freezing conditions and icebergs. Basically it would mean that responding to a Gulf of Mexico-style spill would be impossible.[17]

Beyond that, Professor Wadhams, a glaciologist of Cambridge University, has said that oil spilled in the Arctic would be encapsulated in ice and transported great distances, to eventually thaw and cause terrible disasters around places distant from the original spill.[18]

North Sea Oil West of Shetland

While the oil beds elsewhere in the North Sea are dwindling, BP is starting to drill the Clair oilfield in the Atlantic/North Sea waters to the west of the Shetland Isles, having received approval from the UK government. BP plans to invest £4 billion here. David Cameron, Prime Minister, said:

> We live in a very dangerous and difficult world. We do not want to be over-reliant on energy supplies from difficult and unstable parts of the world. This is great news for Aberdeen and the country and provides a massive boost for jobs and growth.

He added:

> There are some people whom you will never reassure, who quite frankly would probably prefer we weren't recovering oil from any part of the North Sea. I don't think you're going to convince them.[19]

As is so often the case, politicians cannot bring together the three ideas of economic growth, peak oil and climate change. Yes, Clair oil may delay the UK reaching the peak in production/consumption of oil, and will probably help economic growth in Aberdeen, but it will also exacerbate climate change by increasing the emissions of greenhouse gases.

Canadian Tar Sands

Just below the surface of the Canadian wilderness in North Alberta are large stretches of deposits of heavy oil mixed with clay and sand. To extract the tar, oil companies are destroying the boreal forest, gouging out vast amounts of top soil, and turning the landscape into a gaping black pit. Two tonnes of earth have to be dug up and processed to produce each barrel of tar sands oil. Tar sands oil creates three times the emissions per barrel involved in getting crude oil from oil wells.[20]

Greenpeace has been campaigning steadily against this development on the grounds of water pollution, air pollution, toxic effects on indigenous people, destruction of the boreal forest and, ultimately, acceleration of climate change. On the other hand, the

UK government has been battling with nearly all of the other European countries, who are trying to keep this fuel out of the European Union.

Tar sands oil makes no sense for our environment or our climate.

Biofuels

Some of the big oil companies, like the US firm Chevron, are working desperately trying to replace fossil oil with liquid fuels from vegetation.[21] Bioethanol is being made from sugar cane, corn, and more recently switchgrass, and biodiesel is made from vegetable oils such as palm oil. Chevron recognises that:

> Tens of millions of tons of biomass are required annually to produce enough fuel to make a difference, given the global demand for energy.

What it doesn't admit is that an enormous amount of land would be required. An estimate made in 2001 calculated that to produce sufficient bioethanol to keep all the cars in the United States on the road would require virtually all of the existing cropland to be planted with corn or sugar cane. Switchgrass is better, but nevertheless, a report from the American Union of Concerned Scientists suggests that 50 million acres of switchgrass might be needed by the year 2025.[22]

Palm oil is converted into diesel fuel in Malaysia and other countries, but again it is clear that vast tracts of land are needed for this and there has been extensive criticism about the loss of tropical rainforests for palm tree plantations.

An alternative to growing biomass on land is to utilise stretches of water and grow algae that give a form of diesel oil. High yields are being claimed, with rapid growing times, in various experiments. The United States Department of Energy estimates that if algae fuel replaced all the petroleum fuel in the United States, it would require 15,000 square miles, which is less than one seventh of the area of corn harvested in the States in 2000.[23] But this would entail an enormous investment for it to be put into practice, and at present nobody seems too interested.

Many think that cars run by electricity are the answer. They do not produce toxic gases, are quiet and smooth running, and are easier to service than cars with internal combustion engines. Batteries are a problem, though, and regular charging is necessary. But fundamentally, where does the electricity come from? Coal-fired power stations which use fossil fuel and pump carbon dioxide into the atmosphere, perhaps? Or nuclear power stations, with the risks associated with radiation leaks and the basic problem of safeguarding the resulting wastes for several hundred years? The green answers of wind turbines and solar power are unlikely to contribute much energy for transport needs.

Hydrogen is seen as an alternative transport fuel, but it is simply a way of storing and transporting energy by electrolysing water with electricity and producing hydrogen.

The Future

In the year 2000, the UK Highways Agency set up a project to consider what transport might be like in the year 2030. This was the rationale for the project – and the aim:

> Recent concerns about traffic congestion, global warming, and environmental sustainability have highlighted the need to think and plan further ahead.
>
> The aim of Vision 2030 is to develop visions for the mobility needs of people and goods in thirty years' time.[24]

The possibility that oil production/consumption might peak and become prohibitively expensive was not mentioned.

Perhaps it won't have happened by 2030 – but the present evidence is that if it hasn't happened by then, it will only be a few years off.

But even in 2011 (at the time of writing), our government hasn't taken the peaking of oil seriously. The proposal to increase the maximum speed on motorways to 80 mph will use more fuel than if it were to be dropped to 60 mph, and the intention to build more roads in order to help kick-start the economy into growth flies in the face of the pending energy crisis.

No doubt there will be temporary fixes to the problem of providing personal transport, but there is an inevitability about recognising that it will not be long before personal and regular motorised transport is seen as a luxury of times past.

It is far-fetched to suggest that it will once again be the camel for the man in the Middle East desert and the horse for the English farmer, but it is likely that bicycles and legs will become major modes of locomotion for most people, and for those who are infirm it will be cycle rickshaws pedalled by erstwhile taxi-drivers. Public transport without petrol or diesel may use electricity from wave, wind or solar power or perhaps revert to steam, using our still-existent coal reserves. Personal transport may use electricity – but there will be great demands on limited supplies, so it is likely to be an expensive way of getting about.

What seems certain is that few will regularly travel far. Circumstances will dictate the need to live mainly in one's own community.

3

The Inevitable: Climate Change due to Global Warming

Global warming is the greatest challenge the country faces.
—Ed Miliband, September 2010

Scientific Opinion about Global Warming

Wikipedia reports that since 2001, 32 national science academies have issued declarations confirming anthropogenic global warming and urging the nations of the world to reduce emissions of greenhouse gases.[25] They vary in the intensity of their judgements, from the 'incontrovertible' statement of the American Physical Society to the more cautious expression of the Royal Society (of the UK).

In November 2007, the American Physical Society adopted this official statement:

> Emissions of greenhouse gases from human activities are changing the atmosphere in ways that affect the Earth's climate. Greenhouse gases include carbon dioxide as well as methane, nitrous oxide and other gases. They are emitted from fossil fuel combustion and a range of industrial and agricultural processes.
>
> The evidence is incontrovertible: Global warming is occurring. If no mitigating actions are taken, significant disruptions in the Earth's physical and ecological systems, social systems, security and human

> health are likely to occur. We must reduce emissions of greenhouse gases beginning now.[26]

In September 2010, the Royal Society (having been challenged by a few of its Fellows as being unscientifically too dogmatic earlier) said this as part of its statement[27] on global warming:

> There is strong evidence that the warming of the Earth over the last half-century has been caused largely by human activity, such as the burning of fossil fuels and changes in land use, including agriculture and deforestation. The size of future temperature increases and other aspects of climate change, especially at the regional scale, are still subject to uncertainty. Nevertheless, the risks associated with some of these changes are substantial. It is important that decision makers have access to climate science of the highest quality, and can take account of its findings in formulating appropriate responses.

Scientific Opinion about Climate Change due to Global Warming

The Intergovernmental Panel on Climate Change (IPCC) is the leading international body for the assessment of climate change. It was established by the United Nations Environment Programme (UNEP) and the World Meteorological Organization (WMO) to provide the world with a clear scientific view on the current state of knowledge on climate change and its potential environmental and socio-economic impacts. The UN General Assembly endorsed the setting up of the IPCC. Thousands of scientists from all over the world contribute to its work on a voluntary basis. Review is an essential part of the IPCC process, to ensure an objective and complete assessment of current information. Its Fourth Assessment Report on Climate Change,[28] published in February 2007, carried dire warnings to the world:

- Warming of the climate system is unequivocal.

- Most of the observed increase in globally averaged temperatures since the mid-20th century is very likely (>90%) due to the observed increase in anthropogenic (human) greenhouse gas concentrations.
- Anthropogenic warming and sea level rise would continue for centuries due to the timescales associated with climate processes and feedbacks, even if greenhouse gas concentrations were to be stabilized, although the likely amount of temperature and sea level rise varies greatly depending on the fossil intensity of human activity during the next century.
- The probability that this is caused by natural climatic processes alone is less than 5%.
- World temperatures could rise by between 1.1 and 6.4 deg C during the 21st century.
- Sea levels will probably rise by 18 to 59 centimetres.
- There is a confidence level >90% that there will be more frequent warm spells, heat waves, and heavy rainfall.
- There is a confidence level >66% that there will be an increase in droughts, tropical cyclones, and extreme high tides.
- Both past and future anthropogenic carbon dioxide emissions will continue to contribute to warming and sea level rise for more than a millennium.
- Global atmospheric concentrations of carbon dioxide, methane, and nitrous oxide have increased markedly as a result of human activities since 1750 and now far exceed pre-industrial values over the past 650,000 years.

Judgements about Climate Change of Senior Political Figures Worldwide

In the face of this scientific evidence, most senior politicians have made public announcements recognising the need to tackle global warming.

In May 2007, when Nicolas Sarkozy was sworn in as the 23rd President of the French Republic, he described global warming as one of two top international priorities for his term of office. (The other was human rights.)

In November 2008, the UK Parliament passed the Climate Change Act, which requires that carbon emissions are reduced by at least 80% by 2050, compared with 1990 levels. The Labour government's Secretary of State for Energy and Climate Change was Ed Miliband.

Until recently, Prime Minister Vladimir Putin of Russia has joked that global warming would be useful to Russians because they would no longer need their fur coats. But in May 2009, Russia's government quietly made a drastic change to its policy on climate change, accepting that anthropogenic global warming poses severe risks and requires immediate action to limit carbon emissions.

In September 2009, Barack Obama, President of the United States, addressing the United Nations, said that 'if the international community does not act swiftly to deal with climate change we risk consigning future generations to an irreversible catastrophe. The security and stability of each nation and all peoples – our prosperity, our health, and our safety – are in jeopardy.'

(Horrifyingly, many in the US Republican Party dispute the scientific evidence that global warming is caused by human activity.)

Also at the UN General Assembly in September 2009, China's President Hu Jintao committed his country to measurable limits on carbon emissions.

In November 2009, German Chancellor Angela Merkel urged the US Congress and the Obama administration to take bold steps to address global warming, describing climate change as one of the 'great tests' of the twenty-first century.

In March 2010, President Luiz Inacio Lula da Silva signed the Brazilian National Climate Change Policy, which sets out how Brazil will tackle its current and future greenhouse gas emissions and how it will adapt to the impact of climate change. In

September 2011 his successor, Dilma Rousseff, said to the UN General Assembly that her country defends a comprehensive, ambitious global agreement to face climate change within the UN framework.

In December 2010, UK Prime Minister David Cameron praised the United Nations deal to curb climate change that was agreed by 190 countries at the Cancun talks. He called it a 'very significant step forward'.

Three months earlier, Ed Miliband, newly elected leader of the UK Labour Party, said: 'Global warming is the greatest challenge the country faces.' Probably all of the world's leaders mentioned above would agree in terms of their own countries.

Why, then, is there so little sense of urgency in tackling it?

Press Presentation of Scientific Evidence about Climate Change

In 2004, two American social scientists, M.T. and J.M. Boykoff, of the University of California, raised an important issue about the role of the press in presenting scientific evidence about global warming.[29] They studied the coverage of global warming between 1988 and 2002 by four prestige US newspapers: the *New York Times*, the *Los Angeles Times*, the *Washington Post* and the *Wall Street Journal*. This amounted to 636 articles. Starting from the scientific communities' consensus that human activity is the dominant factor in global warming, these were their results:

Articles exclusively discussing human responsibility for global warming	6%
Articles treating human activity as the dominant factor	35%
Articles taking a 'balanced' view of human activity and natural variation	53%
Articles sceptical of human activity and focused on natural variation	6%

Thus, while 35% of the articles reflected the consensus view of scientists and only 6% rejected this view (authored by the 'deniers', as they are now called), over half (53%) of the articles reflected the journalists' canon of giving a balance between conflicting views – seen by the press as scientists on the one hand and deniers on the other. Boykoff and Boykoff argue that the urge for 'balance' in practice leads to a biased coverage of the causes of global warming and, in effect, misleads the readers of these newspapers. It certainly raises an important question about the ethics of reporting what is seen as fact and what is opinion.

The *Guardian*

The *Guardian* probably has the best known answer to this question, in terms of C.P. Scott's maxim that 'facts are sacred, but comment is free'. Of the British daily newspapers, it gives the best coverage of global-warming and climate-change issues. But it allows the facts of science to share some space with the comments of deniers. This is illustrated by these extracts from a *Guardian* interview[30] of Lord (Nigel) Lawson – former Chancellor of the Exchequer – by Julian Glover, when Lawson's *An Appeal to Reason: a cool look at global warming* was published in 2008:

> His argument boils down to two parts: climate change is not the threat we believe and efforts to stop it are doomed and dangerous. Everyone who says otherwise is either lying or ill-informed.
>
> Sipping coffee in the House of Lords, Lawson bristles at the charge that his book is nothing more than an upmarket green ink letter from an ill-informed retiree. . . . At times, though, the mask of rationalism slips. 'I think that the ordinary bloke has an instinctive sense that it wouldn't be too bad if the weather warmed up,' he says, when I question his repeated claim that 'gentle and moderate' warming could turn out to be good for the planet.
>
> Some of the attacks on Lawson are unfair. He has every right to assert his opinions. He is right that scientific predictions of future

> climate change from computer models are inherently unreliable and right to warn that Stern's market-led solution to climate change may not work. But neither of these is to be celebrated.... He does not appear troubled by the thought that he might just be wrong, and everyone else right, and that the consequences of following his advice would be global humanitarian disaster.

Daily Mail

Compare this with an article in the *Daily Mail*, by reporter Julia Wheldon, on 5 March 2007:

> **Greenhouse Effect is a Myth, Say Scientists**
>
> Research said to prove that greenhouse gases cause climate change has been condemned as a sham by scientists.
>
> A United Nations report earlier this year said humans are very likely to be to blame for global warming and there is 'virtually no doubt' it is linked to man's use of fossil fuels. But other climate experts say there is little scientific evidence to support the theory. In fact global warming could be caused by increased solar activity such as a massive eruption.
>
> Their argument will be outlined on Channel 4 this Thursday in a programme called The Great Global Warming Swindle raising major questions about some of the evidence used for global warming.

Curiously, in August 2010, the *Daily Mail* announced that while hitherto sceptical of scientists arguing that global warming is a consequence of human activity it now accepted this position, but then, less than a year later reverted to its scepticism, as this extract from an editorial comment (dated 9 July 2011) demonstrates:

> **Inconvenient Truths**
>
> When the former head of the Civil Service accuses Whitehall of unthinkingly swallowing fashionable theories about global warming, it's time for ministers and mandarins to take notice. For as Lord Turnbull points out, huge uncertainties surround the science of

> climate change. Yet at immense cost, the Government is blindly committing Britain to the world's most ambitious targets for cutting carbon emissions.
>
> Already millions are feeling acute pain, through hidden levies which have contributed to the latest £200-a-year increases in our energy bills.
>
> The Renewables Objective – the European Emission Trading Scheme – the Carbon Emissions Reduction Commitment – the Climate Change Levy – the Carbon Price Floor – all carry huge price tags, which threaten to double energy charges by 2020. Yet the scandal is that these secret extras which add 15 to 20 per cent aren't even itemised on our gas and electricity bills.

Rumour has it that this return to climate change scepticism came after Paul Dacre, editor of the *Daily Mail*, had lunch with Lord Lawson, who chairs a body called the 'Global Warming Policy Foundation'. It is interesting that Lord Turnbull, cabinet secretary (2002–05), who trained as an economist, is a director of this Foundation. Lord Lawson, former Chancellor of the Exchequer (1983–89), read Philosophy, Politics and Economics at Cambridge University and rose to power as a financial journalist. Neither of these men has any background in science, but both are well versed in the polemics of politics!

Does it matter that the *Daily Mail* is sceptical of climate change in the face of very strong scientific evidence? Yes, because over two million people buy it every day. But do newspapers influence the judgements of their readers? There is American evidence that television may influence some viewers.

Impact of Television on Public Opinion: Fox News

Two researchers at Stanford University (Jon Krosnick and Bo MacInnis)[31] analysed data from telephone interviews of a nationally representative sample of 1001 American adults, carried out between 1 and 14 November 2010. Questions were asked about television news viewing and opinions were sought on global warming and its causes, and the possible effects on the US economy of attempts to ameliorate it. Because Fox News, watched frequently by about one third of Americans, was known to have a policy of deep scepticism concerning the scientific evidence about global warming, the analysis separated Fox News watchers from the viewers of other news networks. Krosnick and MacInnis found the following:

> More exposure to Fox News was associated with more rejection of many mainstream scientists' claims about global warming, with less trust in scientists, and with more belief that ameliorating global warming would hurt the US economy.

Nevertheless, they report that:

> Even among the heaviest Fox News viewers, about 50% or more endorse the views of mainstream scientists.

Demonstrating their scientific caution about causality, they conclude:

> It is impossible to discern from these results what causal processes produced the observed relations. One possibility is that exposure to frequent sceptical messages about global warming on Fox News caused viewers to adopt those opinions. A second possibility is that viewers who hold those opinions *a priori* choose to watch Fox News, because it frequently expresses views that agree with their own.... . We suspect [a combination of both].

Power of the Media in Influencing the Public on Climate Change

So, the overwhelming scientific judgement is that climate change is happening and that the cause is predominantly human activity.

Most ruling political figures worldwide accept this judgement and declare climate change must be tackled by their governments. But the measures that they are taking are feeble responses to the gravity of the situation.

Why? Because they are dependent on the support of their electorates, and these are given mixed messages by the media concerning the certainty that man-made climate change is upon us. On the one hand media like the *Daily Mail* and the *Daily Express* in the UK, and Fox News in the US, have editorial imperatives that deny that human activity is responsible for climate change and hence attack any government moves to reduce their nation's carbon footprint, while on the other hand other media outlets, including the 'quality' newspapers, are saddled with an ethic that seeks 'balance' in handling conflict between scientific evidence and contrary opinion.

As a result, any government that tried to enforce the drastic reductions in greenhouse gas emissions that the science tells us are necessary would be out of office at the next election.

John Vidal, Environment Editor of the *Guardian*

Most of the media are failing to inform the public of the dangers ahead which we should be tackling now. But a notable exception is the *Guardian*'s environment editor, John Vidal. He regularly reports on worldwide events of environmental consequence, and has a reputation for scientific accuracy combined with hard-hitting comment. On 14 June 2011 he had a three-page article (in the *Guardian* supplement *G2*), from which I quote:

> **Warning: Extreme Weather Ahead:** John Vidal, 14 June 2011
>
> Tornadoes, wildfires, droughts and flood were once seen as freak conditions. But the environmental disasters now striking the world are shocking signs of 'global weirding'.

> Drought zones have been declared across much of England and Wales, yet Scotland has just registered its wettest-ever May. The warmest British spring in 100 years followed one of the coldest UK winters in 300 years. June in London has been colder than March. February was warm enough to strip on Snowdon, but last Saturday it snowed there. . . .

Vidal then shows that what we had experienced in Britain in 2011, extreme as it seemed to us, was nothing in comparison with other parts of the world:

> Last year, more than 2m sq km of eastern Europe and Russia scorched. An extra 50,000 people died as temperatures stayed more than 6°C above normal for many weeks, crops were devastated and hundreds of giant fires broke out. The price of wheat and other foods rose as two thirds of the continent experienced its hottest summer in around 500 years.
>
> This year, it's western Europe's turn for a mega-heatwave, with 16 countries, including France, Switzerland and Germany (and Britain on the periphery), experiencing extreme dryness. The blame is being put on El Nino and La Nina, naturally occurring but poorly understood events that follow heating and cooling of the Pacific Ocean near the equator, bringing floods and droughts.
>
> Vast areas of Europe have received less than half the rainfall they would normally get in March, April and May, temperatures have been off the scale for the time of year, nuclear power stations have been in danger of having to be shut down because they need so much river water to cool them, and boats along many of Europe's main rivers have been grounded because of low flows. In the past week, the great European spring drought has broken in many places as massive storms and flash floods have left streets in Germany and France running like rivers.
>
> But for the real extremes in 2011, look to Australia, China and the southern US these past few months. In Queensland, Australia, an area the size of Germany and France was flooded in December and January in what was called the country's 'worst natural disaster'. . . .
>
> In China, a 'once-in-a-100-years' drought in southern and central regions has this year dried up hundreds of reservoirs, rivers and

> water courses, evaporating drinking supplies and stirring up political tensions. . . . [Then] a record 30 cm of rain fell in some places in 24 hours, floods and mudslides killed 94 people, and tens of thousands of people have lost their homes.

Across the Atlantic it was the same:

> Meanwhile, North America's most deadly and destructive tornado season ever saw 600 'twisters' in April alone, and 139 people killed in Joplin, Missouri by a mile-wide whirlwind. Arizonans were this week fighting some of the largest wildfires they have known, and the greatest flood recorded in US history is occurring along sections of the Missouri River. This is all taking place during a deepening drought in Texas and other southern states – the eighth year of 'exceptional' drought there in the past 12 years. . . .
>
> In Mexico, the temperature peaked at 48.8°C (119.8°F) in April, the warmest anywhere in the world that month, and nearly half of the country is affected by drought. There have already been 9,000 wildfires, and the biggest farm union says that more than 3.3 million farmers are on the brink of bankruptcy because they cannot feed their cattle or grow crops.

Vidal summarises these extreme events as being indicative of world climate being in 'overdrive' and notes that various international aid agencies were now warning of impending disaster. While sceptics disagree, scientists, cautious as ever, nevertheless expect it:

> Sceptics argue that there have always been droughts and floods, freak weather, heat waves and temperature extremes, but what concerns most climate scientists and observers is that the extreme weather events are occurring more frequently, their intensity is growing and the trends all suggest long-term change as greenhouse gases steadily build in the atmosphere. . . .
>
> While no scientist will blame climate change for any specific weather event, many argue that these phenomena are textbook examples of the kind of impact that can be expected in a warming world. Natural events, such as La Nina and El Nino, are now being exacerbated by the background warming of the world, they say.

The Entitlement to Know What is Happening in the World

In terms of one of the democratic entitlements suggested in the Introduction – lifelong learning opportunities and the right to know what is happening in the world – we need more journalists of John Vidal's calibre reporting in all the various media.

We need journalists to avoid seeking to give their readers a balance between unsupported opinion and scientific evidence, but instead aiming to help people to understand how serious global warming is. People need to know that scientists are cautious but truthful in their utterances. People need to know that time is running out, and they need to demand appropriate action of their elected representatives in reducing our national emissions of greenhouse gases.

Part Two: Conviviality

4

Conviviality: The Alternative to Wealth Creation

I consider conviviality to be individual freedom realized in personal interdependence and, as such, an intrinsic ethical value.

—Ivan Illich (1973)

Capitalism

Capitalism is about private ownership of the means of production of goods and services, and about marketing these in order to make a profit after paying for the labour hired, the equipment utilised, the space occupied and the raw materials needed. In contrast, socialism is about the public ownership of the means of production of goods and services without making a profit after paying from the public purse (i.e. through taxation) for the labour hired, the equipment used, the space occupied and the raw materials needed. Capitalists argue that because of the competitive nature of market forces, private ownerships give the public better goods and services. Socialists argue that this is not so, because the private owner creams off a profit.

I believe that there is a place for both. I am content with food and clothes being sold by private companies, but I want health care and education to be in the public domain.

My concern is not with capitalism as such, but with greedy capitalism, with capitalism that puts wealth creation by the individual above the public good.

I fear that for too many people in the business world of industry, commerce and finance, the major driver of their model of capitalism is greed, manifested as maximising wealth creation. Capitalism need not be like that, but today too often it is.*

I have thought long about this, and of the antithesis of wealth creation, which (after Illich) I call 'conviviality'.

Wealth creation has produced prosperity for many people across the world and misery for many others. Today it can be seen to be the prime agent of man-made global warming, incipient climate change and riches for some and poverty for others.

Wealth Creation

Wealth creation is the prevalent ethos of the macro world of business and of nations. This is a way of living where wealth creation is central – in the naïve expectation that this will continually give greater access to goods and services and hence endlessly improve the quality of life. Wealth creation puts people in competition with each other, and this is seen as the engine of progress that leads to greater affluence.

Historically, wealth creation has achieved remarkable levels of affluence: it has built towns, transport systems, communication systems, schools, hospitals, churches; it has funded great architecture, geographic exploration, scientific discovery; it has filled our shops with desirable goods and made widely available many public services. But also it has led to devastating levels of misery through the greed and hedonism of those who have put wealth

* Jonathon Porritt, in *Capitalism as if the World Matters* (Earthscan 2005), argues that because of 'the biophysical limits to growth' and 'the terrible damage done to the human spirit through the pursuit of unbridled materialism', capitalism must be transformed into sustainable development that adheres to the core values of 'interdependence, empathy, equity, personal responsibility and intergenerational justice'.

creation for themselves above the basic needs of others who are less fortunate. Politically, the struggle to create more wealth has put nation against nation, sometimes leading to war. Today the ethos of wealth creation is pushing the world towards global socio-ecological disaster, particularly through the over-exploitation of natural resources and global warming caused by the excessive production of atmospheric pollutants.

I am one who believes that to ameliorate this situation the richer countries of the world need to contract their economies, while the poorer countries need to expand to the point where the economies of the world eventually converge. To achieve this, countries like ours, rich through successful wealth creation over several centuries (even if we still have substantial pockets of poverty), need a different ethos.

While wealth creation is the current ethos of many businesses and governments, among many families and local communities there is a different ethos and one which could lead us to the global convergence which social justice and ecological necessity demand. I call it conviviality.

Conviviality

Ivan Illich, the South American philosopher, introduced the term conviviality in his book *Tools for Conviviality*,[32] and I have tried to develop it, including ideas from Schumacher's *Small is Beautiful*,[33] so that the adjective 'convivial' and the noun 'conviviality' are given a profound meaning which goes far beyond the jovial to identify the roots of human joy, social justice and ecological sanity.

I see 'conviviality' as a way of living through which people gain quality of life and enjoy happiness by striving to be in harmony with themselves and with their social, cultural and natural environments. For each individual this can be a lifelong learning project; for every society it can be the source of peace, prosperity and sustainability.

Convivial people seek a state of deep and satisfying harmony with their world and through this a joyful meaning to their lives.

- Seeking harmony with their natural environment, they use it for their needs, but try not to exploit it; they strive to conserve the land, its natural resources and the living things which it supports and, seeing themselves as stewards, aim to safeguard the land for future generations.
- Seeking harmony with their cultural environment, they learn from it, savour it, contribute to it, and aim to pass on what they see as worthwhile to future generations.
- Seeking harmony with the social environment of their fellows, convivial people try to cooperate rather than compete; endeavour neither to exploit others nor to be exploited by them; participate in the management of their society through democratic structures; strive to live in concord with all – to love and be loved.
- Seeking harmony with their inner selves, convivial people search for understanding of their own rationality, spirituality and emotions in order to develop their talents effectively; and by trying to use their talents harmoniously in relation to society and the environment, they experience the joy of convivial life.

To varying extents, these attributes are found in families and small communities where members care for each other, care about their local environment, learn the underlying values in school and in relation to those who are close to them, and act altruistically.

If the human world is to survive the disasters that global

warming and peak oil will cause, it is necessary to recognise that this prevailing ethos in the micro-world of many families and small communities is the best way forward for the macro-world of developed countries like ours. It is the ethos of conviviality, where mostly people live in altruistic harmony with each other, support each other, conserve their surroundings and aim to pass on to future generations that which they hold worthwhile. Likewise, most teachers, doctors, nurses, social workers, charity workers, and carers for the elderly and sick, as well as some lawyers, reflect the ethos of conviviality.

How Conviviality Impinges on Politics

To recap: conviviality is a way of living through which people gain quality of life and enjoy happiness by striving to be in harmony with themselves and with their social, cultural and natural environments.

How does this impinge on politics? Politics is a process by which people make collective decisions about the management of their affairs, local, national and worldwide, and this can be conducted either within a 'wealthiest' ethos or within a 'convivial' ethos.

Here are some of the major ways in which conviviality can impinge on politics:

- *Tackling global warming* is a convivial issue because conviviality entails trying to safeguard the earth for future generations and conserving the earth and the living things which it supports. It follows that rich countries must limit consumerism and replace economic growth with a sustainable concern for the quality of life and the well-being of all.

- *Tackling poverty and malnutrition* wherever it exists is a convivial issue because conviviality entails seeking to live in harmony with fellow human beings and so being able to support them in their times of need. It follows that poor countries need to be able to grow their economies – aiming eventually to converge with the reduced but sustainable economies of the presently rich countries. This also gives a convivial reason for supporting fair trade.
- *Aiming for nations to be more or less self-sustainable in food production, energy provision, water availability and other natural resources* arises as a convivial issue because conviviality entails using the natural environment for needs, but not exploiting it; conserving the land; and exercising stewardship of precious resources to safeguard future generations' access to these.
- *Aiming to avoid or reduce conflict* arises as a convivial issue because conviviality embraces the idea of harmony between peoples, trying to cooperate rather than compete, and neither exploiting nor being exploited. This ideal stretches from in-family feuds and workplace bullying to urban riots, terrorism and international warfare.
- *Aiming to replace individualism with community involvement* arises because conviviality includes the idea of harmony with fellows and cooperation rather than competition. It embraces altruism and rejects the 'me-first' culture.
- *Aiming to reduce inequality* arises as a convivial issue because conviviality endeavours neither to exploit others nor to be exploited and embraces democratic ideals of social justice as fundamental aspects of harmony between people. Thus, while a pay differential between the highest and lowest paid of say one to ten may be

necessary to reward effective management, the very high rates of pay in many large companies exploit the low-paid. For these same reasons, the convivial ethos embraces values of honesty, respect and empathy for others.

- *Espousing education which embraces notions of nurture, culture and survival and which is worthwhile, satisfying, joyful and life-long* arises from the notion of living in harmony with one's cultural environment and learning from it, savouring it, contributing to it and aiming to pass on what is seen as worthwhile to future generations; and from the notion of seeking harmony with one's inner self and searching for understanding of one's rationality, spirituality and emotions in order to develop one's talents.

A Worldwide Viable Future in which Economies Converge

These ideas are a key to seeing how a viable global future could evolve. Our descendents across the globe – children, grand-children and beyond – must be able to enjoy what they will perceive as a worthwhile quality of life. To achieve this, the industrial countries of the world should begin to replace the ethos of wealth creation with the ethos of conviviality in national and international life, while the developing countries should use wealth creation to raise the standards of living of their peoples and use conviviality to ensure that these standards are shared by all of them. Thus, rich economies should contract and poor economies expand to the point where they converge.

In order to succeed in this just mission, it needs to be recognised that economic growth (i.e. wealth creation) is a phe-nomenon of societies moving to maturity, and that thereafter economic stability (i.e. zero economic growth) is needed within societies which are convivial; this is obtained through their being socially just, democratically governed, environmentally responsible, and culturally stimulating, and prospering mainly on the renewable resources and produce of their own territories, while trading minimally with each other and supporting one another in times of need.

Combatting global warming and the peaking of oil are the greatest of today's worldwide challenges to industrial countries like ours, while these, coupled with malnutrition and, in places, starvation, are the major challenges to many developing nations. They cannot be tackled in isolation from issues of poverty, economic growth, international trade, and sustainability. These are all relevant to creating a better world.

A better world would avoid wars, famines and eco-catastrophes. It would celebrate the cultural heritages of its peoples, ensure social justice for all, and focus its technological advances on ensuring the sustainability of life on earth.

As humankind becomes wealthier it must begin to eschew the pursuit of further wealth and instead seek for quality of life for all. If we connect the natural conviviality of people with the reality of political action, progress just might be made towards creating sustainable, peaceful and just societies throughout the world.

5

How a Convivial Ethos Could Change Our Society for the Better

A way of life that bases itself on materialism, i.e. on permanent, limitless expansionism in a finite environment, cannot last long.

—E.F. Schumacher, *Small is Beautiful: a study of economics as if people mattered* (1973)

'Conviviality' is described in the previous chapter as a way of living through which people gain quality of life and enjoy happiness by striving to be in harmony with themselves and with their social, cultural and natural environments. Here are eight ways in which this ethos could impact on our society.

They are approaches to the idea that life should be joyful; that people should be autonomous in their decisions and communal in their activities; that people should be able to find satisfaction in developing their talents; that they should relate to their fellows socially and justly; that they should be educated in providing for the necessities of life.

They are not objectives or benchmarks or targets for government – or whatever the latest fad is in management-speak. They are not the stuff of laws or edicts from on high. They are ideas for people to think about, argue over, and develop. They are suppositions that could, perhaps, help to create a better world than that of today, but that doubtless will be held to be hopelessly naïve by those currently in power. But the convivial view is that some of them, one day, may become national aspirations.

[1] Suppose that the production of goods and services is in harmony with the essential needs of consumers, so that there is little over-production and little under-supply. Suppose that, for the workers producing goods and services, their employment is planned in terms of job satisfaction for the worker as much as with a view to profit in the sales. Suppose that for the consumers of goods and services there is sufficient production to satisfy their essential needs, but insufficient to pander to greed.

Industrial society requires workers to specialise in producing goods. In Adam Smith's classic account (*The Wealth of Nations*, 1776)* of the division of labour in pin-making, he identified a number of distinct operations, each carried out by a different operative:

> One man draws out the wire, another straightens it, a third cuts it, a fourth points it, a fifth grinds it at the top for receiving the head ... (p. 12)

Smith had seen a 'small manufactory' where ten men working, 'when they exerted themselves', could make 48,000 pins in a day – an average of 4800 per man.

> But if they had all wrought separately and independently, and without any of them having been educated to this peculiar business, they certainly could not each of them have made twenty ... (p. 13)

He did not seem concerned about the inevitable tedium of such work! A century later, Karl Marx argued that, as a result of this division of labour, workers become alienated or estranged from their work and from its product. Michael Argyle, in *The Social Psychology of Work* (1972),[34] noted that sociologists had identified four different aspects of workers' alienation – namely:

---

* Citations are from the Oxford World's Classics edition of 1998.

- ***powerlessness*** – lack of control over management policy, the conditions of employment and the work process;
- ***meaninglessness*** – inability to see the purpose of the work done and how it fits into the whole production process;
- ***isolation*** – lack of belonging to a coherent working group; and
- ***self-estrangement*** – inability to regard work as a central life interest or means of self-expression, which leads to a depersonalised detachment while at work. (pp. 225–226)

The Industrial Revolution resulted in the rapid creation of wealth, and the standard of living in the industrial countries soared for nearly everyone to levels previously only known by the very rich. (There is, certainly, still relative poverty in the industrial countries, but this can be attributed to mal-distribution of resources occasioned by greed of the powerful rather than to overall shortage). But now that the transition has been made to a high level of affluence, the manufacturing processes characteristic of the industrial age may no longer be needed. Adam Smith, in his delight in showing that far greater numbers of pins could be manufactured by his advocacy of the division of labour, doesn't seem to have considered that more pins might be produced than consumers wanted. To extend the metaphor, nor did he visualise a situation where the bosses of the pin factory would use every means they could to persuade people to buy more pins.

Today our shops, particularly supermarkets, are overfilled with foodstuffs. Retailers buy from food producers more than they can sell: in 2008 the Sustainable Development Commission (a government watchdog) estimated that retailers in the UK throw away 1.6 million tonnes of un-purchased food each year. Beyond this, households buy more than they can eat: the government department DEFRA estimated in 2008 that households wasted 5.3 million tonnes of food waste that could have been avoided.

Likewise, clothing shops are overfilled with clothes, shoe shops with shoes, furniture stores with furniture, electrical stores with electrical goods, and so on. Notwithstanding the pressures of advertising and the abundance (until recently) of easy credit, the production of goods exceeds their consumption and so, every few months, shops have to try to clear their shelves by 'fantastic' offers in cut-throat sales – in order to make room for a new generation of products. In turn, when households buy new, they throw out old – even though the latter may still be quite serviceable.

Turbo-consumerism, as Neal Lawson has described this phenomenon, damages the lives of the workers engaged in production through pressure to cut costs, cut labour, and work long hours, while it manipulates the lives of consumers so that they want more. As Lawson has said in *All Consuming* (2009):[35]

> Government action is required to establish a post-consumer world. First, the state can stop harmful consumer practices by restricting advertising, taxing luxury goods and rationing scarce resources. Second it can help foster good buying behaviour and activity by making ethical shopping and recycling easier. Finally, through our democracy, we can create spaces in which markets are restricted and effectively regulated, so we can be citizens, not just consumers, to help us forge more durable and satisfying identities as workers while providing us with the time and money to live more autonomous lives. (p. 242)

[2] Suppose that fewer mass-produced goods are manufactured and that more people experience the joy of making their own homes, furniture and clothes, and of cooking their own food. Suppose that, in consequence, fewer people work in factories. Suppose that goods produced are robustly designed for a long life, to be mended if possible rather than replaced when broken, and recycled when beyond repair.

The do-it-yourself movement demonstrated to millions of people that there is intense satisfaction in craftwork at home. Enthusiasts build their own furniture, home extensions, garages, even houses, boats and caravans. Others continue the long-practised crafts of their forebears in food preparation and preservation, beer and wine making, knitting, weaving and dress-making, gardening and home decorating. Yet many others lack the confidence to do these things and fail to recognise the personal joy from doing them. If local communities possessed communal workshops and kilns it would be possible to considerably extend the craft activities which people can learn and carry out for themselves. It is true, of course, that engaging in these activities requires a certain amount of wealth in order to buy tools and materials.

It is possible to conceive of some manufacturing industries withering away as domestic crafts take their place. Obviously certain kinds of manufacturing are going to be needed in order to sustain domestic craft activity – for example, of small machine tools, screws, hinges, plastic fittings, planed wood and plastic surfaces. Likewise, factories for the manufacture of televisions, recorders, refrigerators, cookers and deep freezers are going to be needed, for few people are likely to construct their own. The convivialist does not seek to domesticate all forms of manufacture, but simply to change the balance in an attempt to raise not the affluence of society, but the quality of life of its members. The convivialist believes that providing ample opportunities for developing the self-reliance of the domestic craftsperson is a way to enhance the quality of life. Obviously schools have an important part to play in this.

Where manufacture is necessary, the convivialist would look for robust designs which are easily serviceable, easily repaired and long lasting. In present-day industrial society, the phrase 'built-in obsolescence' leads one to believe that certain manufactured goods are designed to wear out within a planned, short period in order to ensure that the consumer buys another and so maintains the wealth-creating function of the manufacturing enterprise.

It isn't only the worker who can be alienated at the workplace. The rest of the community may be as well. This is powerfully expressed by Robert Pirsig (1984) in a passage in *Zen and the Art of Motorcycle Maintenance*:[36]

> You go through a heavy industrial area of a large city and there it all is – the technology. In front of it are high barbed-wire fences, locked gates, signs saying NO TRESPASSING, and beyond, through sooty air, you see ugly strange shapes of metal and brick whose purpose is unknown, and whose masters you will never see. What it's for you don't know, and why it's there, there's no one to tell, and so all you can feel is alienated, estranged, as though you didn't belong there. Who owns and understands this doesn't want you around. All this technology has somehow made you a stranger in your own land. Its very shape and appearance and mysteriousness say, 'Get out.' You know there's an explanation for all this somewhere and what it's doing undoubtedly serves mankind in some indirect way but that isn't what you see. What you see is the NO TRESPASSING, KEEP OUT signs and not anything serving people but little people, like ants, serving these strange incomprehensible shapes. And you think, even if I were part of this, even if I were not a stranger, I would be just another ant serving the shapes. So the final feeling is hostile. (pp. 16–17)

[3] Suppose that technology is not used to save human labour, but to assist its use in satisfying ways which neither exploit people nor pollute the earth, nor wantonly consume non-renewable resources.

Two men were watching a huge excavator rapidly digging a vast hole in the land. One said, 'In place of that machine there could be work for a thousand men with picks, shovels and wheelbarrows.' His companion replied, 'Or for a million men with teaspoons.' This expresses succinctly the moral problem of technology: the problem of knowing where to draw the line on technological development and of finding a sane balance between two extremes, one of which is absurd to the wealthist and both of which are absurd to the convivialist. In wealthist terms, the size of the digging machine is decided by the economics of the project: the manager looks for the cheapest way of digging the hole. Can we conceive of an alternative where the decision as to how to dig the hole is based on consideration of the greatest good for the greatest number? Nobody wants to dig with teaspoons, but suppose that a thousand unemployed people were given the choice of decent pay in employment with picks and shovels, or living on the dole and watching machines do the digging: which would they choose?

Of course, the question needs to be asked, 'Why do we need the hole?' If the answer is 'To build a community swimming pool', the response may be quite different from that for 'To build a missile silo'. The wealthist manager sees no difference between the two – his task is to get the hole dug as quickly and cheaply as possible – but the convivialist manager recognises that the workforce is likely to be more sympathetic to the swimming pool and may gain greater satisfaction from the labour involved in digging it.

But it may be better to employ a hundred people using small digging machines than a thousand with picks and shovels, if this eases the work and best serves the needs of the community. This may be the appropriate balance between the big and the small.

[4] Suppose that industrial countries like the UK stop trying to become more affluent, stop consuming a disproportionate share of the earth's resources, and begin to become mainly self-sufficient within their own territory.

The British import-export economy is currently structured this way. In order to purchase the food and raw materials needed to supplement our indigenous supplies and thus sustain our way of life, we export manufactured goods and, increasingly, professional and financial services. On the international market we buy grain, fruit and mineral ores, for example, and pay for these by selling chemicals, machine tools and weapons. Just half of the food we buy in our shops is home grown; the rest has to be imported – and paid for by our exports.

The cycle of importing raw materials, turning them into manufactured goods, using some ourselves and selling the rest overseas, and using the overseas profit to buy not only more raw materials but also the additional food we need was the strategy of success of the UK for over two centuries. It helped us become an affluent society, in which all of our people, even those deemed 'poor', have reached higher standards of living than many in the rest of the world. Over the same period many other countries have done likewise. But now our industrial pre-eminence is challenged by more countries, particularly those in Asia. Their industrial rise was based on cheap and abundant labour, but now the key factors are technological knowledge and, in most cases, a national ethos expressed in determination to succeed in the world's markets. Japan, for example, produces more graduate engineers and trained technicians than the UK, and each company's workforce has a cultural system involving universal loyalty to the enterprise – something rarely found in the UK.

Is it not time for the UK to become much more self-sufficient and for us who live here to live primarily on the resources of our own land? We have the amassed wealth and the technology to do this; but what is lacking is the political will. Unfortunately, our politicians, responding to what they perceive as the desires of the people and the pressure of the ballot box, continue to argue that we need more affluence and that therefore we must capture foreign markets; but in the long term, the days of this strategy are inevitably numbered.

As a nation we are better nourished, housed, educated, cared for, protected against pain and disease, and entertained than any of our predecessors on this island and than most of the rest of the world. Why do we want more? Why are we not prepared to consolidate what we have and to establish a sustainable society so that our grandchildren and their grandchildren can also enjoy a high quality of life? Also, why do we not share what we have more equitably amongst ourselves?

At present our society is endangered by a dearth of political and world-moral education. Most of us are grossly ignorant of the realities of the world: of the exploitation of the 'South' by the 'North', of the squalor and poverty in which so many people exist, of the widespread inhumane behaviour of man towards man. Few have sufficient knowledge to comprehend the awful epigram (perhaps epitaph) that was coined some years ago: *The Earth has cancer and that cancer is man.* Most of our newspapers trivialise world events and titillate us with small celebrity scandals and heinous crime reports. Television programmes occasionally bring the harshness of the world into people's homes, but the dead bodies of starvation or revolution seem no more real than those of the regular diet of thriller films. Some television does seek to help people to understand the world rather than view it, but sadly it attracts only small audiences. We blunder forward in ignorance of the major problems of a changing world.

[5] Suppose that there is less competitive advertising, so that people are under less persuasion to become more affluent.

Wealthist economic theory centres on the concept of growth: it requires a steady growth in consumption, fed by a parallel growth in production, to maintain the process of accretion of wealth.

In order to achieve steady growth in consumption, the public has to be motivated to buy more goods, and so wealthist society employs specialists in persuasion who, using artistic skill and psychological knowledge, encourage people to buy, use, throw away and buy again. By subtle – and not-so-subtle – advertising techniques, the public are manipulated into being dissatisfied with older fashions and into striving to be 'one up' on their neighbours. TV and radio commercials, posters on hoardings, and magazine and newspaper announcements subject us to a constant barrage of persuasion about washing powders, beers, motor cars, mortgages, perfumes, clothing . . .

Over fifty years ago, Vance Packard, in *The Hidden Persuaders* (1957),[37] warned western society in these terms:

> Large scale efforts are being made, often with impressive success, to channel our unthinking habits, our purchasing decisions, and our thought processes by the use of insights gleaned from psychiatry and the social sciences. Typically these efforts take place beneath our level of awareness; so that the appeals which move us are often, in a sense, 'hidden' . . . This depth approach to influencing our behaviour is being used in many fields and is employing a variety of ingenious techniques. It is being used most extensively to affect our daily acts of consumption. (p. 11)

More recently, Gannon and Lawson, in a Compass report entitled *The Advertising Effect* (2010),[38] see much advertising as damaging to the Compass vision of the good society:

> The goal of advertising is not the creation of happiness and consumer fulfilment. Instead the purpose and consequence seems to be the creation of a mood of restless dissatisfaction with what we have got and who we are so that we go out and buy more. Advertising is no longer there to inform about the advantages of one product over a rival. (p. 8)

In addition, they recognise that it is damaging the earth:

> Advertising is contributing not just to our levels of debt and happiness but also to the unsustainability of the planet. (p. 14)

Gannon and Lawson conclude that much better regulation of the advertising industry is needed.

> Advertising regulations now need to catch up with the reality of the advertising effect on us and our planet. This is not the announcement of a war on advertising but a sensible rebalancing of competing interests: those of profit making with society making and environmental sustainability. (p. 22)

The advent of Internet shopping has led to the major companies developing databases of customers and their purchases so that, using electronic devices called 'cookies' (which the companies can put on customers' computers without their knowledge), selected advertisements can appear on the customers' screens to encourage new purchases. Internet shopping has facilitated the secret monitoring and manipulation of consumers.

Suppose it were possible to take a national decision to stop seeking higher levels of affluence, then it would become evident that competitive advertising is inappropriate. 'Competitive' advertising refers to announcements promoting one brand over another; it can be distinguished from 'informative' advertising, which seeks to advise the public of new products, but not to persuade them to buy already well-known goods.

One of the problems of such a decision would be that alternative ways of funding television and radio programming that is currently financed by advertising revenue would be needed; there would also be a need to support magazines and newspapers which are currently heavily dependent upon the advertisements they carry.

[6] Suppose that more people find the time, opportunity and desire to play sports, take exercise, write poetry, sing, make music, paint, make films, act, and generally do their own thing in active rather than passive ways.

Why is it that in contemporary society many people watch football, cricket and tennis on television, but few play these games themselves? Why is it so rare to hear people singing or making music when clearly so many people enjoy listening to music? Why is it unusual to see anybody sketching or painting pictures? Most homes have pictures on the walls, but these are nearly always mass-produced reproductions and rarely originals. Why do so few people take part in local dramatics when so many enjoy drama on television, cinema screen and stage?

The answer lies in the nature of wealthist society, which is concerned always with *the excellence of the product* (measured as its wealth) rather than with *the pleasure of the process.* This results in the majority of people in a wealthist society being passive because they know that their standards of playing football, cricket or tennis, of singing or playing a musical instrument, of sketching and painting, of dramatic acting, are inferior to those of the professionals, the experts and the specialists. In a competitive world they have learned that to win or to be acclaimed is what matters, and for those who cannot achieve excellence it is better never to try. Wealthist society encourages passivity in all of its members except the small elite who excel.

Convivialists value the process of playing games, of making music, of painting, of acting – as sources of harmony. Sports entail relating to others and developing oneself, painting entails relating to the cultural and perhaps physical environment, and so on. Each entails developing harmony within oneself through the satisfaction of engaging in the active process. The sports writer Grantland Rice expressed it as follows:

> For when the one Great Scorer comes to write against your name,
> He marks not that you won or lost, but how you played the game.[39]

Attitudes towards activity and passivity develop in one's youth. In our early years we are all active; as we grow up we may remain active, or begin to adopt a passive attitude. In this, the experience of our school education is significant.

Education

In a wealthist society education is geared towards the creation of wealth, and so emphasis is placed on gaining knowledge and skills in order to obtain a 'good' job. The wealthist claims that moral and aesthetic values are not neglected and that sufficient opportunities are available for creative and physical activities in the educational programmes of schools; nevertheless, these are seen as peripheral to the main objective of preparing for employment. The wealthist wants the less able – as judged by assessment tests – to acquire such knowledge and skills as will enable them to work under the direction of the more able in the industrial and commercial pursuit of wealth. The wealthist wants the more able to acquire such knowledge, skills and values as will prepare them to be the inventors, technologists, managers and accountants of industrial-commercial society.

When wealth creation is no longer the prime aim of society, the educational system will be able to shift from an emphasis on knowledge, problem-solving skills and wealthist values to one on expressive and creative arts and related moral and aesthetic values. Convivialist education is concerned with the development of the individual as an autonomous being, who can be self-reliant and who can live in harmony with self, with others and with the environment. Schooling can contribute to the development of young people's natural creativity, but today this only happens to a significant extent for a small proportion of the population.

Convivial education requires a different kind of teacher from the didactic instructor demanded by much of the education of a wealthist society. The convivial teacher needs to be a student among students: one who promotes activity by being seen as active – as thinker, writer, artist, musician, craft worker, actor, sportsperson, etc. More than any other members of a convivial society, teachers need to be in harmony with their fellows, with their environment and with themselves – so that through their example and leadership others may learn to be convivial.*

[7] Suppose that people learn more about how to live in harmony with their own self

A number of years ago an advertising hoarding showed a young woman executive, smartly dressed, and the caption, 'London this morning, Paris tomorrow morning, the Daily Mail every morning'. Someone had scrawled across the bottom with a thick felt-tip pen 'And valium every evening'. In Britain today, many families have at least one member who regularly takes tranquillisers – to reduce the personal tension which seems to arise from the stress of living in a wealthist society.

It is said that Samuel Pepys, living in the seventeenth century, would meet his friends at two or three of the clock – but would not have comprehended the idea of meeting someone at half past two, or quarter to three. These terms have been commonplace for well over a hundred years, with the hour further divided into five-minute intervals marked clearly on most timepieces. But more recently, digital clocks and watches, aided by the insistent urgency of time signals broadcast on radio stations, have caused us to measure our lives in minutes. An unknown cynic, parodying Kipling, wrote:

> If you can fill each unforgiving minute
> With sixty seconds' worth of time well run,
> Yours is the world and everything that's in it,
> And a coronary at fifty-one.

Today there is a tremendous sense of rush. The labour-saving, and therefore cost-cutting, practices of industrial and commercial managers spill over into every other aspect of wealthist society.

---

* See my book *Education for the Inevitable: schooling when the oil runs out* (Book Guild, Brighton, 2010).

Packaged meals are advertised as ways of saving time, airlines advertise their routes as being the fastest way of getting from A to B, cars are advertised in terms of their rapid acceleration and top speed (irrespective of the legal upper speed limit), and the *Reader's Digest* abridges popular novels so that the story can be completed faster. Yet what does this saving of time achieve? Instead of savouring the many facets of life, many people seem anxious to gallop past as fast as they can – and in the process, subject themselves to constant stress.

Most people are familiar with the sense of stress that is felt as a personal state of tension in which one is braced for action and ready to respond to what may be round the corner. As such, it is a natural reaction to extra physical or mental demands and is an important mechanism for dealing with the vicissitudes of life. But after the event, one needs to calm down to a more quiescent level of existence. This is what many people today seem to find difficult to do. It may be true that the stress mechanism evolved in primitive people at a time when intense physical activity – fighting or running away for survival – followed the state of tension, and that this strenuous activity dispelled the state of tension and returned the body to its normal state. Certainly some people find that exercise such as jogging, playing squash, or working out on machines in a gym has a relaxing effect after a period of tension. This line of argument suggests that because most of today's problems do not entail intensive physical activity it is much more difficult to return to the quiescent level; in consequence, some people live all the time in a state of stress – or constant strain, as it is often described.

As an alternative to intense physical activity, deep relaxation can be achieved through such practices as yoga, transcendental meditation or autogenic training, for example. These are techniques which anyone can learn, provided there is an appropriate teacher available.

[8] Suppose that there is more respect for persons, and that domination of one by another is eschewed.

Conviviality entails harmony between people, which requires human beings showing respect for each other. This respect is embraced – though often forgotten, in various forms, by all of the world's religions. It is present in the socialist credo 'Equality, liberty, fraternity'. It can be seen in the Declaration of Independence of the United States, in the recognition that fellow human beings have the same entitlement as oneself to 'life, liberty and the pursuit of happiness'. And it is in the United Nations Charter.

However, though few wealthists will agree, it is difficult in a wealthist society for this respect to be nurtured between all people, because wealth-creating activities entail a concentration of wealth in the pockets of some at the expense of others. Wealthist activities such as creating a market, persuading someone to buy, maintaining demand, and making a profit tend to cause salespersons to treat purchasers with less human respect than, say, they accord their own families. Wealthists' reasons for not selling poor-quality goods tend to be that they have to abide by the law and are concerned that purchasers may not return if the goods are inferior to what they can get elsewhere. The moral argument – that it would be wrong to sell shoddy goods, because this would be disrespectful to the purchaser – is rarely heard. Indeed, moral arguments are often treated in a wealthist society as naïve, and the business person sees nothing wrong in taking as big a profit as possible from whoever can be persuaded to do business with him or her.

Perhaps the clearest demonstration of the wealthist's disregard for moral arguments lies in the armaments industry, the very existence of which must represent the epitome of lack of respect for other persons. Large numbers of technologists in the industrial countries are engaged in devising and manufacturing weapons to kill and maim people (it is said that half of the world's physicists are employed in the armaments industry). Most arms traders are motivated by profit, not by patriotism or belief in a cause.

Wealthism seems to lead to the domination of one person by another in hierarchies of power. In the private sector, the operative is told what to do by the charge hand, who receives orders from the foreman, who is directed by the manager, who works to targets set by the works director, who is answerable to the managing director, who reports to the company chairperson. In the public sector, the clerk is told what to do by the section head, who is directed by an executive officer, who receives orders from the district manager, who is answerable to an assistant secretary, who reports to the permanent secretary. Sometimes these relationships are based on mutual respect, but too often they entail the senior person dominating the junior one and in some cases enjoying the exercise of power. The wealthist justification for a hierarchy of power is that it is needed in order to be effective in creating wealth or in maintaining a system which conserves wealth.

Since conviviality is fundamentally concerned with harmony, the idea of one person dominating another is unacceptable to the convivialist. Thus, if an institution is to be convivial, it is necessary to establish relationships between the members based on mutual respect and not domination of one by another. It follows that convivial institutions need to be small, in order that the members can know one another and therefore develop this mutual respect. In the words of E.F Schumacher, 'small is beautiful'.

Part Three: Rethinking for the Inevitable

6

Rethinking Income and Taxation

There is enough in the world for everyone's need: but not enough for everyone's greed.

—Mahatma Gandhi

Britain in Grip of 'Worst Ever Financial Crisis'

On 7 October 2011 the above was the front-page headline of the *Guardian*. It was quoting the governor of the Bank of England, Sir Mervyn King, as he announced that his institution was injecting £75 billion into the British economy – in what is called 'quantitative easing', but what for most of us means 'printing more bank notes'.

Like most people, I have only a rudimentary understanding of our national finances, but I recognise a crisis when it comes. Larry Elliott, writing in the *Guardian* on the same day,[40] gave an account of the crisis current at the time of writing. I quote part of his article:

> Here's a potted version of the story so far. Progressively over the past three or four decades, the UK economy has been pulled out of shape. There has been less emphasis on making things, greater reliance on financial services. Manufacturing has been hollowed out, the City has grown immeasurably bigger. Finance is more important to the UK economy than it is for the US, Germany, France or Japan.

> In the boom years before 2007, the economy had three main motors of growth: a speculative bubble in the City, a speculative bubble in the housing market, and a growing public sector that was dependent on bubble tax receipts.
>
> Then the lights went out. The housing market sagged. Consumers decided they had too much debt. The banks belatedly became a lot more choosy about the people to whom they would lend. Demand collapsed as the credit machine ground to a halt and getting the economy going again has proved mightily difficult.
>
> Initially, the response was to rapidly slash short-term interest rates, from 5.5% to 0.5%, the lowest level in the Bank's history. Because the banking system had been so damaged by the downturn, this was seen as insufficient, so the Bank stepped in with its first tranche of quantitative easing.
>
> It pumped £200bn into the economy between early 2009 and 2010 in an attempt to drive down long-term interest rates, which are determined by movements in the financial markets rather than by central bank technocrats.
>
> Fiscal policy – tax and spending decisions – was also relaxed, with a temporary cut in VAT and fast-tracking of infrastructure projects. That, coupled with tumbling tax receipts, punched a big hole in the government's finances.
>
> For a while, it seemed the patient was responding to the medicine. By the time the coalition government was formed in May 2010, Britain was growing at around 1% a quarter, and Osborne and Cameron decided that the economy had enough juice to cope with the biggest fiscal squeeze since the IMF laid down the law to Jim Callaghan's government in 1976.
>
> They thought the private sector was robust enough to take up the slack left by a retrenching public sector, while exports would compensate for the weakness of domestic demand caused by consumers spending more prudently. It was the wrong call.
>
> The economy has flat-lined since last autumn, and the Bank fears worse may be ahead this winter.

As I have made clear in earlier chapters, I believe that 'flatlining' (i.e. zero economic growth) is what is needed in the UK (and other affluent countries) on ecological grounds. I doubt whether the current crisis will mark the end of economic growth in the UK, but it will inevitably happen after the next crisis, or the one after that.

The transition from a growth economy (even a faltering one) to a steady-state economy is going to be traumatic for everybody. This chapter describes fiscal policies that could ease the transition, essentially by narrowing the gap between rich and poor. They are convivial policies rather than wealthist ones: no doubt naïve, but less naïve than the expectation that growth will continue for ever!

Narrowing the Gap between Rich and Poor in the UK

The following scenario for re-orientating the UK economy entails citizen's income, a fair minimum wage and a maximum take-home-pay. It would give some financial support to the economically inactive and end child poverty, at a time when economic growth is surely coming to an end, and when global climate change and peak oil demand drastic financial readjustments by a rich developed nation such as ours.

To implement this scenario will require a chancellor of the exchequer of the calibre of Lloyd George. In 1908 he introduced old-age pensions for poorer people aged 70 and over. In order to pay the £16 million a year needed, his budget in 1909 increased income tax and excise duties, put new taxes on cars, petrol and land, introduced a supertax of 6d in the pound for those earning more than £5,000 a year, increased death duties on the estates of the rich and taxed profits made from the sale of property. The poor were winners and the rich losers: it represented an exemplary reduction in inequality. The House of Lords rejected this budget, but after a long struggle Lloyd George won. His 'Limehouse speech'[41] to 4,000 people in the East End of London deserves wide reading still. Subsequently, the Parliament Act of 1911 restricted the Lords' power to block House of Commons legislation.

The proposals of this chapter will be daunting to any politician and will certainly require an extensive public campaign to persuade the electorate that it is a viable way into the uncertainty of the future. My view is that it is the *only* viable approach to tackling the gathering storm.

'What Do You Want Out Of Life, What Does It Mean To You?'

In March 2009 the Labour Party's website invited contributions to a noticeboard of what one would want to say to Prime Minister Brown, President Obama and the other G20 leaders before their April meeting. This was mine:

> Recognise that the end of economic growth in the developed countries of the world may save the planet from global warming; celebrate it by introducing a fair minimum living wage and a maximum take-home pay and replace the complexities of most benefit and tax credit systems by a universal citizen's income (financed by the state from taxation), which gives fair support to the out-of-work and those who can't work – like children, students, voluntary workers, the elderly, the infirm, and those who support family members at home.
>
> Don't try to rebuild the old economic system – create a new one of stability, sustainability, and succour for the poor of the world based on a convivial ethos instead of wealth creation. We are now the richest generation which has ever lived on this planet – let us act wisely to safeguard the quality of life of our grandchildren and of theirs.

This chapter outlines three measures which would facilitate the development of a steady-state economy:

- a small citizen's income for all citizens in the UK as a non-means-tested right;
- a minimum living wage, with legislation that precludes anyone being paid less;
- a maximum limit to take-home pay, with taxation that prevents anyone gaining more.

Some of the possible consequences are discussed: these measures would end child poverty, support those who lose their jobs, encourage voluntary work, and bring politicians' obsession with economic growth to an end. They would also cause outrage among the wealthier members of society!

They would reduce the 'inequality' in our society and in consequence, as argued convincingly by Wilkinson and Pickett in *The Spirit Level: why more equal societies almost always do better* (2009),[42] should improve our health, reduce mental illness, improve education, reduce crime, and, by increasing the trust between people, help build the vibrant communities that will be needed to cope with future environmental problems.

But beyond these, this scenario, by reducing the amount of money available for consumer spending, would make our carbon footprint smaller and move Britain towards the targets put forward by Nicholas Stern in *A Blueprint for a Safer Planet* (2009),[43] involving reducing the carbon emissions of developed countries by 20–40% of our 1990 emissions by 2020, and by at least 80% by 2050.

Undoubtedly these measures would be rejected by the majority of economists who believe there is no alternative to perpetual economic growth; they would infuriate the rich and the powerful in our society and would worry those in the middle ranges of income, but they should be welcomed by the majority of the population if they come to recognise the security that they offer them. Once it is understood that these measures would not only protect both the unemployed and those who are at risk of becoming unemployed, it should be the case that there would be more votes for the measures than against them. Certainly they deserve the support of all of us who worry about the world that our grandchildren will live in. But they will require patient explanation and not the rejection of shoot-from-the-hip-and-ask-questions-afterwards politicians, nor banner headlines of 'rubbish' from the tabloid press.

They bring into sharp focus the question for all of us: 'What do you want out of life, what does it mean to you?'

On 18 March 1968, at the University of Kansas, Robert F. Kennedy said:[44]

> Too much and too long, we seem to have surrendered community excellence and community values in the mere accumulation of material things. Our gross national product … counts air pollution and cigarette advertising, and ambulances to clear our highways of carnage. It counts special locks for our doors and the jails for those who break them. It counts the destruction of our redwoods and the loss of our natural wonder in chaotic sprawl. It counts napalm and the cost of a nuclear warhead, and armored cars for police who fight riots in our streets. It counts Whitman's rifle and Speck's knife, and the television programs which glorify violence in order to sell toys to our children.
>
> Yet the gross national product does not allow for the health of our children, the quality of their education, or the joy of their play. It does not include the beauty of our poetry or the strength of our marriages; the intelligence of our public debate or the integrity of our public officials. It measures neither our wit nor our courage; neither our wisdom nor our learning; neither our compassion nor our devotion to our country; it measures everything, in short, except that which makes life worthwhile.

His challenge to economic growth was made at a time before man-made climate change was widely recognised as the major threat to our existence. Yet one is responsible for the other.

Mike Hulme, in his enigmatic book *Why We Disagree about Climate Change* (2009),[45] says:

> [W]e need to see how we can use the idea of climate change – the matrix of ecological functions, power relationships, cultural discourses and material flows that climate change reveals – to rethink how we take forward our political, social, economic and personal projects over the decades to come. (p. 362)

Anyone who sees the film *The Age of Stupid*[46] will recognise that we in the developed world have a lot of rethinking to do.

Vince Cable, before he became a minister in the Conservative/ Liberal Democrat coalition, wrote at the end of his carefully argued book about the origins of the world economic crisis, *The Storm* (2009), the following:[47]

> It should be possible, despite public spending constraints, through the generous but efficient provision of public goods, genuinely redistributive taxation and strong, solid safety nets for working families and pensioners, to remove extreme inequalities of wealth, income and opportunity; to recreate a sense that the country is a community; and to repair some of the damage that this great storm has wreaked. (p. 157)

What follows suggests how this might be done while preparing us to tackle the root causes of global climate change.

Citizen's Income

In 1985 *Resurgence* published an article of mine called 'National Benefit'.[48] It advocated a low-level basic payment, as a citizen's right, to every man, woman and child in the country, and paid for from general taxation. The magazine carried a similar article by a Belgian writer, and the editor described the two contributions as 'perhaps an idea whose time has come'. Many years later, revisiting this idea with the benefit of Google, I realised that many others had worked on this idea, going back at least to Thomas Paine in 1797.

In a pamphlet called *Agrarian Justice*, Paine argued that

> the earth, in its natural uncultivated state … was the common property of the human race.

However, in order to develop agriculture effectively, private ownership of the land had become inevitable. Nevertheless, the basic needs of all humanity must be provided for by those with property, because at some time in the past they have taken the land and should pay those for whom originally it was common land. The idea didn't catch on anywhere, with the exception, late in the twentieth century, of Alaska (because of the vast revenues from local oil).

I think few people would pursue Paine's argument of social justice based on one-time common ownership of the land, but today there is, I believe, a powerful argument for social justice in terms of contemporary disparity between the rich and the poor and the random chance of being born to rich or poor parents. A steady-state economy must involve an effective mechanism for equitable sharing of wealth across the nation.

In Europe in 1986 the Basic Income European Network (BIEN) was founded (renamed Basic Income Earth Network in 2004), committed to the idea of a universal basic income as an entitlement of citizenship not related to work or charity.

A prominent advocate has been Philippe Van Parijs, of Louvain University, who wrote in 2004:[49]

> Entering the new millennium, I submit for discussion a proposal for the improvement of the human condition; namely that everyone should be paid a universal basic income (UBI), at a level sufficient for subsistence. . . .
>
> By universal basic income I mean an income paid by government, at a uniform level and at regular intervals, to each adult member of

> society. The grant is paid, and its level fixed, irrespective of whether the person is rich or poor, lives alone or with others, is willing to work or not. (pp. 11–12)

He argued in terms of social justice (freedom for all), policy (reduction of unemployment and poverty), feminism (protection from the potential tyranny of husbands, bosses and bureaucrats), and green politics (environmental concerns linked to economic growth and the alienation generated by industrial society). And he presented a delightful ethical argument in support of the idea:

> True, a UBI is undeservedly good news for the idle surfer. But this good news is ethically indistinguishable from the undeserved luck that massively affects the present distribution of wealth, income and leisure. Our race, gender and citizenship, how educated and wealthy we are, how gifted in math and how fluent in English, how handsome and even how ambitious, are overwhelmingly a function of who our parents happened to be and other equally arbitrary contingencies. . . . Such gifts of luck are unavoidable and, if they are fairly distributed, unobjectionable. A minimum condition for a fair distribution is that everyone should be guaranteed a modest share of these undeserved gifts. Nothing could achieve this more securely than a UBI. (p. 23)

Introducing a universal entitlement to a subsistence income, paid by the state using money generated from taxation, is likely to be an essential factor in moving from a growth economy to a steady-state economy and in trying to create a sustainable society.

The recognition that everyone is a worker, irrespective of whether they are working for an employer or are working unpaid for family or community at home or on an allotment, is important. If a factory or office closes, there is a financial safety net for those no longer employed by the factory or office. In these circumstances, a government does not have to be alarmed at workplace closures, nor need to give export licences for unethical goods such as armaments in order to keep people employed. If high street purchases of goods or the sale of services overseas fall there is no need for panic measures by government. It means that more people move into the unpaid part of the economy. If the numbers involved are appreciable then it becomes the job of the Chancellor of the Exchequer to 'balance the books' by either increasing the levels of taxation or decreasing the quantum of citizen's income. Either measure might lead to economically inactive people seeking paid employment and so, in principle, the system would adjust to maintain equilibrium.

In the UK in 1984 the Basic Income Research Group (BIRG) was set up to promote debate on the feasibility and desirability of a citizen's income. In 1992 it was renamed the Citizen's Income Trust – a registered charity with a website[50] and a regular newsletter. It is affiliated to the international Basic Income European Network (BIEN, as mentioned above), which it helped form.

In 2007 the Citizen's Income Trust published on its website a useful description of this concept, from which the following is quoted:*

> A Citizen's Income (CI) is an unconditional, automatic and non-withdrawable payment to each individual as a right of citizenship. This scheme would phase out as many reliefs and allowances against personal income tax and as many existing state financed cash benefits as possible, and replace them with a Citizen's Income paid automatically to every man, woman and child.
>
> The Citizen's Income attack on poverty is three pronged. Such a scheme would
>
> - end the poverty and unemployment traps, hence boosting employment;
> - provide a safety net from which no citizen would be excluded;
> - create a platform on which all citizens are free to build.

* Another account of this idea is given in Clive Lord's *A Citizens' Income: a foundation for a sustainable world* (2003).

> A Citizen's Income would encourage individual freedom and responsibility and help to
>
> - bring about social cohesion. Everybody is entitled to a Citizen's Income and everybody pays tax on all other income;
> - end perverse incentives that discourage work and savings.
>
> A Citizen's Income would be simple and efficient and would be:
>
> - affordable within current revenue and expenditure constraints;
> - easy to understand. It would be a universal entitlement based on citizenship that is non-contributory, non-means tested and non-taxable;
> - cheap to administer and to automate.
>
> A Citizen's Income varies only with age; and there will be additions for disability.

These ideas have been fleshed out by the Citizen's Income Trust in some detail, demonstrating the simplicity of the proposals, their concept of social justice and how they would reduce the opportunity for fraud. Every citizen, as a fundamental entitlement, would receive from the state a small independent income, irrespective of any paid employment. It would be tax free and not subject to any means test.

> A Citizen's Income scheme would co-ordinate the income tax and benefits systems. A single government agency would credit the Citizen's Incomes automatically and recoup the cost via income tax levied on all income rather than running separate systems of means testing, benefit withdrawal, and taxation. Instead of different rules for claimants and taxpayers, everybody would be treated alike.
>
> Each week or each month, every legal resident would automatically be credited with the Citizen's Income appropriate to his or her age. For most adults this could be done through the banking system, and for children it could be done through the bank accounts of their parents. For adults without bank accounts special provisions would be necessary. Citizen's Income supplements would be paid to older people and those with chronic disabilities, but there would be

> no differences on account of gender or marital status, nor on account of work status, contribution record, or living arrangements.
>
> Tax-free and without means test. The Citizen's Incomes would be tax-free and without a means test, but tax would be payable on all, or almost all, other income. This is necessary in order to finance the scheme.

How would it be financed? The Citizen's Income Trust envisages a reorganisation of income tax embracing employees' national insurance contributions, with everybody paying tax on earnings. The rate of tax would depend on the level of citizen's income. The higher the citizen's income, the higher the tax rate; thus, the citizen's income level and the income tax rate required to fund it would be inherently linked and therefore stable. It could, of course, also be financed by alternative tax systems – such as a land or wealth tax.

In effect, this idea can be seen as extending the existing entitlements of child benefit and old-age pension to all ages. Two of its great merits are that it would provide a level of dignified subsistence to those without the opportunity for paid work, and it would be symmetrical between men and women, married or single, since it would be paid to the individual, not the household or family.

What is remarkable is that the calculations of the Citizen's Income Trust suggest that it could work within the current national budget. The following figures applied to the year 2006–07. If weekly citizen's income payments had been £34 for 0–18-year-olds, £45 for 19–24-year-olds, £57 for 25–64-year-olds, and £114 for those aged 65 years and over, with £2 billion for administration, the costs would have totalled about £191 billion. Adding together 2006 levels of social security spending, tax relief and allowances, and the administrative costs of the Department for Work and Pensions (DWP) and HM Revenue & Customs (HMRC), the actual national expenditure was £201 billion.

It is difficult to put these figures into a comparable context, but in 2011 (at the time of writing) the following were weekly entitlement payments by the state:

- child benefit for the eldest child up to age 16: £20, and for each other child: £13;
- job seekers' allowance for unemployed 16–25-year-olds: £51 (for up to 182 days);
- job seekers' allowance for 25-year-olds and older: £64 (again, for up to 182 days);
- basic state pension for 65-year-olds and older: £101.

Each of these benefits is hedged in by a complex administration which might lead to greater – or sometimes smaller – payments. Thus, pension credit may lift the basic pension to £137, and income support may provide the long-term out-of-work with £67. As many commentators have said, state benefits are a bureaucratic minefield – but while benefit fraud gets a high media profile, it is clear that unclaimed benefits are very much larger than stolen ones.

In February 2010, twenty-seven leading charities in the UK called on the government (Labour at that time) to improve the take-up of welfare benefits and tax credits. The Chief Executive of Citizen's Advice, David Harker, claimed that up to £10.5 billion of means-tested benefits and £6.2 billion of tax credits remain unpaid every year. He said:

> The benefits and tax credits system is extremely complicated and the reasons people don't claim what they're due are complex, ranging from simply not knowing about the benefit concerned, to being put off by what can sometimes seem a very daunting process, to feeling that the amount they gain will be negligible. But all too often they are missing out on substantial amounts of extra cash that could make all the difference between getting by or going under.[51]

Citizen's income would avoid these difficulties because it would be paid directly, as a citizen's right, to every living person. The Citizen's Income Trust recognises that some transitional measures will be needed; for example, 'civil servants at Her Majesty's Revenue and Customs and the Department for Work and Pensions will have to be retrained or made redundant'.

This all seems a highly convivial approach to recognising that in the life span of everyone, from birth to death, there are periods when support from the state can be an important – and sometimes vital – contribution to their quality of life. Moreover, in a rich society such as ours, with a stable system of government and well-developed administrative structures, the provision of such support as citizen's income is an affordable contribution to social justice, which should be the common right of all people irrespective of where they are born, or who their parents are, or what fortune or misfortune dominates their lives.

Those who would denigrate this idea as a 'charter for scroungers' should recognise that very few people seek idleness as a way of life. A desire for both work and play is hard-wired into nearly everybody – as is discussed in depth in Chapter 7. As expressed earlier, the key lies in the question 'What do you want out of life, what does it mean to you?'

Minimum Income Level

The National Minimum Wage Act of 1998 was one of that particular Labour administration's greatest achievements and was, of course, opposed by the Conservatives and Liberal Democrats. It set a minimum limit to the hourly rate that any worker in the country should be paid (although those under 21 years old are paid less), and at the time of writing, this rate is £6.08 per hour. It has steadily been increased in order to keep pace with inflation.

The Joseph Rowntree Foundation has conducted a number of research studies into the needs and costs of different households, and has devised what it terms a minimum income standard:

> A minimum standard of living in Britain today includes, but is more than just, food, clothes and shelter. It is about having what you need in order to have the opportunities and choices necessary to participate in society.[52]

In 2008, the Foundation[53] concluded that the then minimum wage of £5.52 per hour for a single person aged over 21 was too low and should have been 21% higher, at £6.88. Recently it has shown that in rural areas a higher rate is needed than in most urban places, mainly due to the costs of transport compared with urban living.

A campaigning group called Citizens UK[54] works to a current (2011) rate in London of £8.30 an hour, and outside London of £7.20 an hour. It accredits companies who agree to pay their workers at least this amount (recalculated every year), which the campaign considers sufficient to enable every worker to earn enough to provide themselves and their dependents with the essentials of life.

Clearly it is important that every worker is able to 'provide for the essentials of family life', and the Rowntree work shows a valuable way in which the amount that is necessary can be calculated. It is also clear that in different parts of the country different 'minima' should apply. There is much to be done in establishing fairness across the country.

The Gap between State Income and Earned Income

Suppose that the Rowntree minimum standard of living (MSI) is £7 per hour for a single adult person. Someone being paid at this level for a 35-hour week would earn £245. Now suppose that the citizen's income, for male or female aged between 25 and 65, is £64 per week (i.e. at the present job-seeker's allowance – but with no conditions attached, no bureaucracy and continues indefinitely). For someone with no paid employment it isn't much – but it is a guaranteed income.

It is a very long way below Rowntree's MSI, and might be termed a 'minimal subsistence' level. As such, it could hardly be described as a 'scroungers' pay out. If there are opportunities for paid work, a person's income could be supplemented without the present hazard of the 'benefit trap': every hour worked would enhance their income.

If every citizen is receiving £64 per week as citizen's income, the MSI could be reduced to £5.17 per hour, since working a 35-hour week at this rate, together with the CI, would bring in £245.

Clearly there needs to be a substantial gap between unconditional income from the state (CI) and the minimum standard of living (MSI) – otherwise, there might be insufficient tax-paying earners to fund the CI! The levels of CI and the extent of this gap would need to be matters for political debate and regular review.

Maximum Income Level

Many of the chief executives of industry and financial so-called masters of the universe receive levels of remuneration which many of us consider to be obscene. How can anyone deserve to be paid £1 million or more – as was the case for 11,000 people in the UK in 2006–07? These people tell us, of course, that they deserve it because of the risk-taking that they are engaged in – and today we know that some of them weren't even clever enough to realise that the credit bubble must eventually burst. They say that their pay is the going rate for their level of work, and add that they will leave the country if they don't get it. Well, the risk taken in this scenario is to *let them go!*

I put the case for distinguishing sharply between gross salaries plus bonuses and take-home pay in a letter in the *Guardian* on 19 August 2009:

Justice Demands Curbs On High Pay

Your correspondents' call for a maximum wage linked to a minimum wage is right. (It is time for action on excessive pay. 17 August)

Before the very rich squeal too loud, we should ask whether it is the gross income that gives them the craved esteem of their fellows, or the take-home income. The fact is that everyone's view of prestigious salaries and bonuses is quoted as gross and not net. So, if this is the testosterone of the higher echelons of the business world, let them be paid these gross sums, glory at the level, boast about it, but pay tax which reduces it to the chosen national maximum! Provided, of course, that the tax authorities can track them down and ensure that people who claim citizenship, make their money here, use our infrastructure, and enjoy our national culture, pay their taxes here in full.

Couple this with citizen's income (paid to all, financed by those in paid employment) and we will have an economic system sustainable into the distant future which by reducing inequality will begin to resolve many of our social and environmental problems. These measures could be such that across the nation more people gain than lose. So it should be possible to enact such changes in a democracy!

The radical proposal here is that nobody should have a take-home pay of more than 10 times the take-home pay of the lowest paid. If the lowest paid have, in Rowntree's terms, what is needed in order to have the opportunities and choices necessary to participate in society, then anyone with two or three times that should be in clover, and to have ten times should be the height of affluence.*

* Professor John Hills, in his *Inequality and the State* (2004), using British Social Attitudes data, showed that in 1999, on average, people thought that the ratio of pay of an unskilled factory worker to the chair of a large corporation should be 1:6.25.

Ten times the Rowntree MSI of £13,000 per year is nearly £130,000. The proposal is that this should be the ceiling for take-home pay before standard tax. This should be the maximum for anyone in the country. (It needs to include bonuses, investment income etc. Since the Inland Revenue should know what any individual is receiving, it should be no problem to ensure that taxation keeps the take-home pay below this maximum.) Call the amount paid on anything above this the 'ceiling tax', as distinct from the 'standard tax' paid by every earner.

So, anyone whose company pays them £1,000,000 a year pays £870,000 in ceiling tax, and then the standard tax (whatever the rate is) on the £130,000.

To most people, it is remarkable that anyone actually needs as much as even £100,000 a year to enjoy a good quality of life. What is certain is that fast cars, over-heated swimming pools, frequent flights to exotic holiday resorts, luxury hotels and many other of the trimmings of the very rich put undue pressure on the environment – and need to be curtailed if we are to reduce our carbon footprint and begin to save the world from overheating. It can also be argued that, through the media, they debase our national culture by suggesting impossible aspirations for others.

In November 2011 the independent High Pay Commission, set up by the left-wing pressure group Compass and the Joseph Rowntree Charitable Trust, published its report 'Cheques with Balances: why tackling high pay is in the national interest'.[55] The chair, Deborah Hargreaves, introduced the report with these words:

> As Britain enters times of unparalleled austerity, one tiny section of society has been insulated from the downturn. That is the top 0.1% of earners, with company directors in particular continuing to enjoy a huge annual uplift in rewards. . . . The public is rapidly running out of patience with a system that allows those at the top to enrich themselves while everyone else struggles to make ends meet.

The report shows the ratio between the 'lead executive total earnings' and the company's average pay in 2009–2011 for the following companies:

Lonmin	113.1
Lloyds Banking Group	75.0
Barclays	75.0
BP	63.2
GKN	47.7
Reed Elsevier	38.4

And the comparison is with the 'company average pay', not, as argued here, with the Rowntree minimum standard living wage.

The Commission ducked the issue of promoting the idea of a limit to this ratio, but made twelve recommendations which should make issues of executive pay more transparent and keep concerns about high pay in the public eye.

What Happens if the Cost of Citizen's Income is such that the Budget can't be Balanced?

The scenario figures given above are, of course, no more than plausible guesswork. The only fixed points are the level of minimum wage and the level which the net income may not exceed.

One of the annual tasks of the Chancellor of the Exchequer would be to determine the quantum of citizen's income and, to keep pace with any inflation, the actual levels for the minimum and maximum levels. In other words, as now, the Chancellor would need to balance the budget.

Suppose that the numbers of the economically inactive rise appreciably. The Chancellor would need to reduce the quantum to balance the budget, and the likely result would be that more economically inactive people would seek jobs and become employed. So the system would slowly adjust to maintain equilibrium.

Taxation

One of the strange anomalies of our tax system is that people tend to think of the standard rate of income tax as 20% whereas, because of national insurance payments, it is actually 32% (i.e 20% + 12%) of income up to a threshold of £35,000 per year, which rises to 42% (40% + 2%) above that threshold, and then to 52% (50% + 2%) if one's annual wage is greater than £150,000. There would seem to be a lot of sense in the proposal of the Citizen's Income Trust that national insurance contributions and income tax should be merged and handled, as citizen's income would be, by the Inland Revenue.

There are at present some 300,000 people in the UK who are paid an annual wage (including bonuses and other benefits) of over £130,000 a year. We can expect that they would not welcome the idea of a ceiling tax which reduced their income to £130,000, which would then be subject to whatever rate of income tax is in force. The Gandhian argument that there is sufficient in the world for each one's need, but not for each one's greed may not impress them. No doubt they will shout that this is 'revolution' – and indeed it is – but a bloodless one that still leaves them with a considerably larger take-home wage than the majority of their fellow citizens. Perhaps they will remember that it was David Cameron, Conservative Prime Minister, who said, 'We are all in this together.' Certainly among their number will be many of the most powerful people in the land – but numerically they are a very small minority who may have to yield to the democratic will of the majority of the people.

Reducing Inequality

Fundamentally we can expect that measures such as these would reduce the inequality in our society.

The Spirit Level: why more equal societies almost always do better, by Richard Wilkinson and Kate Pickett,[56] shows how many factors in national life are influenced by the gap between the best-off and the worst-off. They quote UN statistics showing that the ratio of average take-home pay of the 20% worst-off to the 20% best off is 1 to just under 4 in the Nordic countries of Finland, Norway and Sweden, 1:7 in the UK, and 1 to nearly 9 in the USA.

In a remarkable series of graphs, they show the relationship in many of the developed, industrialised nations between inequality of income and an impressive list of social parameters. For those to whom the following social parameters apply, each of the three above-mentioned Nordic countries show a much better quality of life than either the UK or the USA:

- Levels of trust between members of the public
- Health and social problems
- Status of women
- Births to women aged 15–19
- Use of illegal drugs
- Infant death rate
- UNICEF index of child well-being
- Obesity in children
- Children's experience of conflict
- People in prison
- Social mobility between generations

Wilkinson and Pickett put forward careful arguments showing that it is income inequality in society rather than actual levels of income that exacerbates these social parameters. First they consider why social anxieties have increased dramatically in the UK and in the USA over the last half century:

> A plausible explanation is the break-up of the settled communities of the past. People used to grow up knowing, and being known by, many of the same people all their lives.... People's sense of identity used to be embedded in the community to which they belonged, in people's real knowledge of each other, but now it is cast adrift in the anonymity of mass society. Familiar faces have been replaced by a constant flux of strangers. As a result, who we are, identity itself, is endlessly open to question. (p. 42)

In such a situation, how much income one appears to earn and how much wealth is displayed by one's house, car, material possessions and overseas holidays compared with others living in the same street, or at work, becomes an important marker of social status. The wider the inequality in society that results from the disparity between the incomes, the more 'rungs' there are on the ladder of social status and the more disparate society becomes.

Wilkinson and Pickett examine each of the social parameters listed above and give plausible explanations of how they may be linked to social inequality arising from income inequality.

We cannot be absolutely sure that by reducing the gap between the rich and the poor the quality of life would change on all of these social parameters, but such a change is sufficiently likely to justify basing national policy upon it. Certainly Wilkinson and Pickett think so, for they write:

> ... if Britain became as equal as Finland, Norway, Sweden and Japan levels of trust might be expected to be two-thirds as high again as they are now, mental illness might be more than halved, everyone would get an additional year of life, teenage birth rates could fall to a third of what they are now, homicide rates could fall by 75 per cent, everyone could get the equivalent of almost seven weeks extra holiday a year, and the government could be closing prisons all over the country. (p. 261)

This is the kind of change in UK society that could be expected if the ideas of this chapter were adopted.

Suppose Fewer People Earned Wages and More Worked Voluntarily

At first sight this looks like a recipe for disaster, since the economically inactive are supported by the wage-earning tax payers. But if Wilkinson and Pickett are right, reducing the gap between the rich and the poor and thereby increasing levels of trust in society would appreciably reduce the national expenditure on health services and penal systems, and so the overall national budget could be stable with fewer wage earners.

Political discourse today is obsessive about wage earning contributing to economic growth. For example, there is pressure on young single mothers to go out to work and to hire someone to look after the child. When this happens there are two people contributing to the gross domestic product in place of none. But suppose the woman would prefer to look after her child herself: citizen's income for her and for her child should enable this to happen. To the dismay of most economists, her decision would not aid economic growth. But is economic growth a proper aim for a rich country?

Political discourse today is also obsessed with the idea of *hard-working* people. Labour first changed its concern with the needs of *working* people to the needs of *hard-working people*, and the Conservatives have followed suit. Why should people work hard? Isn't it for them to decide? The political answer is that if they don't work hard the nation will not have economic growth. But, again, is economic growth a proper aim for a rich country?

In Ecclesiastes,[57] the philosopher asks, 'What do we gain from all our work?' In the mists of uncertainty, he concludes:

> I realized that all we can do is to be happy and do the best we can while we are still alive. All of us should eat and drink and enjoy what we have worked for. It is God's gift.

Whether one is theist, agnostic or atheist, the message is the same: it is the quality of life that matters. Since work is part of life for nearly everyone, it follows that the quality of work matters.

Looking again at contemporary political discourse, it tends to be forgotten that the notion of work applies much more widely than only to wage-earning work. Mothers looking after young children are working (unpaid) from the time the child awakes until the time the child goes to sleep, and even then the mother is on the alert. Family members caring for sick or infirm relatives are working (unpaid). The allotment owner is working (unpaid) to provide food for the family. The neighbour who takes food to the elderly person next door is working (unpaid). And, of course, anyone engaged in study is working (unpaid). Beyond this are the organised forms of voluntary work (unpaid) of charities, drive-patients-to-the-doctor schemes, hospital visitors, prison visitors, election workers, and so on.

Work is part of the stuff of life. For some it is an intolerable grind, but for most people it is a way of relating to others and provides a sense of achievement, which, however small, is worthwhile. For most it is a source of contentment and satisfaction. (When this is not so, either managers or politicians have a case to answer.) It is a deep-set part of our culture. People want something worthwhile to do with their lives. The concern that citizen's income would turn people into layabouts and idlers is ill-founded. Very very few people want to stay in bed most of the day. They may not want to work long hours, but they want something satisfying to do and, supported by citizen's income, that may well be voluntary work. Since citizen's income in this scenario is less than what is seen in the Rowntree study as being necessary for a 'socially acceptable standard of living', there will be an incentive for many people living alone to seek paid work, but for couples with young children it will be much more practical than now for one of the parents to be a wage-earner and the other a house-parent, and they will probably swap roles from time to time.

The argument is that an economy could be created in which it is not necessary for every able-bodied person to be a wage-earner. This idea, perhaps outrageous, is developed in the next chapter.

The Ideas of this Chapter Would Reduce Our Carbon Footprint

The economic theories that all boats – big and small – are raised by the incoming tide, and that as the rich get richer, some of the wealth trickles down to benefit the poor, are not true for the UK today. The use of the gross domestic product (GDP) as a measure of national success is no longer appropriate. It is of no significance to our well-being if the GDP falls – indeed, if, as a result of levels of interpersonal trust increasing, the prison population declines and hospital admissions fall (among other factors), the GDP *will* fall! People are coming to realise that it is quality of life that matters, not economic growth.

But there is more to the end of economic growth than outdated economic theory. Almost inevitably, economic growth enlarges a nation's carbon footprint. If we are to tackle global warming effectively, the UK – and all other of the developed industrial countries – must consume less, travel less, and transport goods less – in other words, we must all spend less and be less avaricious.

Sadly, and potentially catastrophically, our previous government of the left and the present one of the right believe Britain should spend its way out of recession in order to re-establish economic growth. In contrast, the Archbishop of Canterbury, Dr Rowan Williams, in his 2009 Easter message,[58] called on consumers to curb their appetites. He said:

> The present financial crisis has dealt a heavy blow to the idea that human fulfilment can be thought about just in terms of material growth and possessions.

The wage levels suggested here, while hopefully sufficient for a fair quality of life, would inevitably lead to less consumption of goods, less travel, and less transportation of goods, and thus reduce our carbon footprint. Britain needs to do this not only as its contribution to reducing global warming, but as a starting point for persuading the rest of the developed world to follow suit. But in the process, the workers who produce the goods and provide the services we consume will experience contractions in employment. A monumental re-orientation of society will ensue. This is why citizen's income is so important – to protect those who lose their paid employment.

Of course, there will still need to be sufficient wage-earners in order to provide the tax revenue for citizen's income, as well as to pay for health care, crime prevention, education and all the other demands on the nation's purse. Getting this balance right by determining the quantum, as discussed earlier, is the function of the Chancellor of the Exchequer and the Treasury, but, as this book argues, they must start from the premise that economic growth is over and a gentle decline in gross domestic product is to be welcomed. Quite a mindshift!

While the provision of citizen's income will provide the means of sustenance for families where the breadwinners are out of paid work, the challenge for our society and its government will be to realign paid work more closely with the basic human needs of food and energy production and community life and service.

Naïve? Yes.

Would enhance the quality of life? Yes.

Could happen? Yes – if the scenario of citizen's income and minimum and maximum wage was implemented. Hopefully, with an increase in interpersonal trust, people would gain quality of life more from community interactions and less from material possessions.

Requires a major cultural change? Undoubtedly. Predominantly in the business world – but bringing with it great opportunities. Families are more attuned to these notions.

Would reduce our carbon footprint? Yes, substantially.

The scenario, in the context of these aspirations, provides a powerful way of responding to the threat of global warming. Ecological concerns for the future provide the most important justification for the scenario.

Great Ideas, But Who Will Support Them?* Yes, the Green Party[59]

Suppose that a Chancellor of the Exchequer, after the Budget speech to Parliament, said this on television to the nation – from a venue in Limehouse, in the East End of London:

> My fellow citizens, in putting forward this radical proposal for citizen's income, this revolutionary proposal for a maximum wage, and this essential proposal for a sufficient minimum wage, I am simply proposing that in the future no one in this country of ours shall be impoverished because of those amongst us who have, by ability or by chance, so ordered our societal structures that they gain a disproportionate share of the annual income of our nation.
>
> We are the richest people that have ever lived on this island, richer than our parents, and much richer than our grandparents, but somehow we have allowed too much of these riches to be acquired by a few. Our forefathers struggled for all to be able to vote so that they could play their part in the affairs of the nation. It is now our

* Having drafted this (in October 2011), I turned, in hindsight belatedly, to the Green Party website and found that it advocates the three measures suggested here: citizen's income, a living minimum wage (of 60% net national average earnings) and a maximum wage (not exceeding ten times that paid to the lowest-paid worker).

turn to struggle for all to have a fair share of the income of the nation. The quality of life of our children and grandchildren is at stake. These measures should eliminate child poverty – long an ambition of government – and also protect the elderly and the disabled.

But also it will ensure that those who are unfortunate in losing their jobs because of the vicissitudes of the markets and those who for one reason or another have not sought paid work, will have a modest income sufficient to keep a roof over their head and the wolf from the door. That we can do this is a measure of the richness of our country and our concern for social justice.

The social scientists tell us that by narrowing the earnings gap between the rich and the poor one of the great characteristics of past generations in this country will return. Trust between people will grow. Suspicion of others will dwindle and, in consequence, communities will thrive. The evidence from countries like Norway, Sweden and Finland, where the earnings gap between rich and poor is much less than ours, is that by introducing measures which reduce that gap, there will be improvements in physical and mental health, less crime, fewer problems with young people, and in general a better quality of life.

But there is another, and perhaps even more important, reason for welcoming these proposals. And here I have to ask you to put your thinking caps on, for at first sight it is not obvious. Many people who have been at the better end of the spectrum of earnings, will find that they have less spending power. They will have sufficient for the necessities of life and for some luxuries, but not at the level to which they have become accustomed. But before they give vent to violent feelings at how this change is affecting them I hope they will come to recognise that by reducing their consumption of goods and energy they are reducing their carbon footprint. By spending less (because they have less to spend) they will be making a significant contribution to tackling the threat of global climate change.

It is, of course, all of us that have to try, individually and collectively, to reduce our carbon footprint. During World War Two our forebears were confronted with posters on public transport asking, 'Is your journey really necessary?' Today we should be asking a broader and more personal question, 'Is my expenditure really necessary?' In a land of plenty, like ours, it is a difficult question to answer. Perhaps we should see it in the context of something that Gandhi said, 'There is enough in the world for each one's need, there is not sufficient for each one's greed.'

Britain began the industrial revolution and today we are, hopefully, starting another revolution which, by spreading through the developed nations of the world, will cause our demands on the environment to contract, and, by helping the less developed nations to raise their standard of living and eventually converge with ours, will ensure that the world's grandchildren, and theirs, will enjoy a satisfying quality of life unsullied by catastrophic climate conditions.

And so, my fellow citizens, in putting forward the biggest change in the economic arrangements that have ever come before this nation, I echo the words of an American President by saying, ask not what this budget means to you, but see how this budget will raise the quality of life for all.

Steep Learning Curve or Precipitous Social and Ecological Decline

I have little doubt that these ideas will be seen by many as extremely naïve. No doubt some of my figures err. Undoubtedly the consequences of implementing the ideas would have major impacts on various elements of the economy which can hardly be predicted. Nevertheless, they are put forward from the following convictions:

(1) That economic growth in a rich country like ours cannot be allowed to continue because it promotes potentially catastrophic climate change;
(2) That, as a generation richer than any of our predecessors, we should in social justice succour the poor;
(3) That no senior executive can deserve more than ten times the pay of the lowest paid;

(4) That by reducing inequality in our society, the quality of life of all will rise;
(5) That our economic ideas must adjust to the ecological demands of the planet; and
(6) That we owe it to our grandchildren and theirs to sort out the mess that we have made.

In other words, we, the general public, and our political leaders have either a steep learning curve or a precipitous social and ecological decline ahead of us.

7

Rethinking Work and Communities

And they shall say, this land that was desolate is become like the garden of Eden; and the waste and desolate and ruined cities are become fenced, and are inhabited.
—Ezekiel 36:35, King James Bible

Unemployment is an Incurable Phenomenon

As long as records have been kept, there have been substantial numbers of people who have sought work in vain. As Figure 4 shows, in the UK in the 1950s and 1960s, they numbered around 2% to 3% of the potential workforce; the figure rose to nearly 5% in the 1970s, shot up to almost 12% in 1984, peaked again in the 1990s at 10%, and dropped to around 5% in the early years of this century, but it is now climbing – reaching 8.1% in August 2011, and amounting to 2.5 million people.[60]

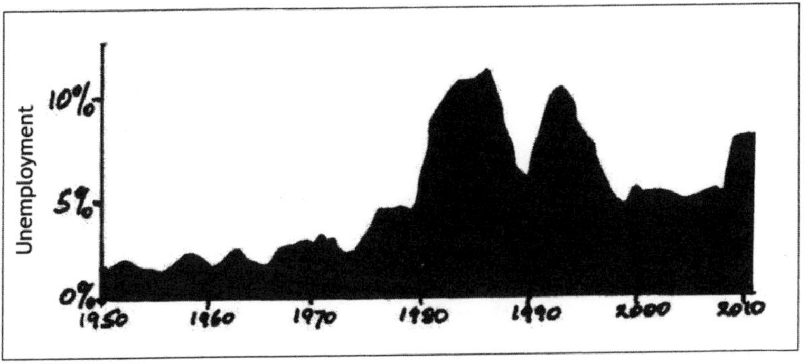

Figure 4. Unemployment in the United Kingdom, 1950–2011

Of these 2.5 million, 867,000 had been out of work for longer than six months, and 722,000 were under 24 years of age. Politicians argue about the reasons for these levels of unemployment and policy makers try to find ways of reducing them, but none grasp the nettle: lack of paid work for some of the fluctuating number of people who seek it is an incurable phenomenon. The evidence suggests that inevitably there will be people looking for work and unable to get it. It is more difficult in some parts of the country than in others, but everywhere there are people failing to find paid work. This matters because it eats into the souls of would-be workers and their families.

Difficult as it is, we need to accept as fact the truth that in many parts of the country in the foreseeable future it is never going to be possible for all of the workforce to be in paid jobs. In accepting this unpalatable truth, we need philosophically to ask each other: 'What do we want out of life – for ourselves, our children and our grandchildren?'

The first of the citizens' entitlements that I put forward earlier involves the right to have work opportunities that provide sufficiently for needs, that are personally satisfying and that are not over-demanding of personal time.

Is this unattainable for some? It is only when we closely examine the concept of work that there is a glimmer of hope for those with little expectation of gaining paid work. But first let us survey the current scene.

For too long we have been led to believe that affluence is what is needed in order to achieve the goal of happiness, and that affluence is achieved through economic growth. This is only true up to a point – and one which as a society we have long ago passed. We have become miserably acquisitive. We have harnessed our lives to wealth creation, along with its connotations of greed, beggar-my-neighbour, self-interest first, and measuring everything in terms of money. Now, as discussed in Chapter 1, economic growth itself is under challenge.

Unemployment across Britain

A report in July 2011 from Sheffield Hallam University by Christina Beatty and Steve Fothergill, entitled *Tackling Worklessness in Wales*,[61] describes the lack of jobs in Wales, but similar arguments will appertain in England, particularly in the North and the Midlands:

> One-in-six of all adults of working age in Wales are out-of-work and on benefits. In some Valley authorities this rises to one-in-four. . . . Even on favourable assumptions . . . there seems little prospect of reducing worklessness to acceptable levels over the next ten years.

These authors recognise that while the private sector has made considerable efforts to generate new jobs, nevertheless it

> has a mountain to climb to deliver new jobs on the scale that is needed, and it seems unlikely to get much beyond the foothills.

In consequence, they argue for the Welsh government to invest in a massive job-creation programme for which, they calculate, the economics would be 'surprisingly positive'.

Figure 5, depicting unemployment across Britain , averaged for July 2009 to June 2010, puts unemployment in parts of Wales at 14% or one in seven – though the situation in Wales may have worsened since then.

The Office for National Statistics published this chart showing unemployment rates in the English regions and in Wales and Scotland. While it may be interesting to ponder the reasons why some regions are worse off than others, this pulls attention away from the naked fact that, throughout the country, there are vast numbers of people without paid employment. What to do about this is the real issue?

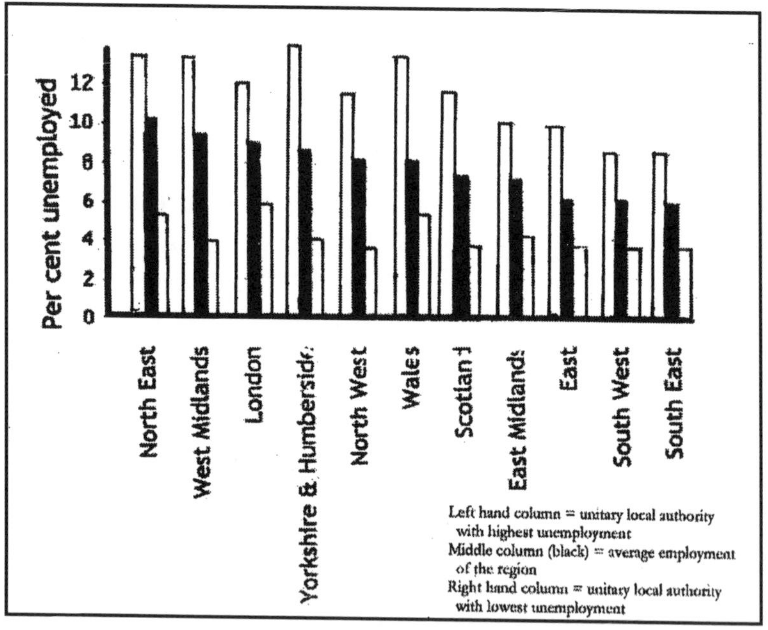

This is how to read the chart. In the North East (for example), the unitary or local authority with the highest unemployment has 13.5% unemployed, the authority with the lowest has 5.5%, and the average unemployment for the region is 10%

Figure 5. Unemployment in Britain, July 2009 to June 2010.
Source: Office of National Statistics (redrawn)

Job Creation – But What Kinds of Jobs?

The issue which those who argue for massive job-creation programmes do not address is this: what kinds of work are the out-of-work going to be offered? What is it that they can do which society needs? How worthwhile are the new labours?

Do we need or want more people turning small pieces of slate into ornaments to give to relatives as presents? Do we need or want more people producing tailored birthday cards emblazoned with words like 'To my Darling Step-Grandfather'? Do we need or want more people making exotic decorations to hang on Christmas trees? Do we need or want more people in call centres asking to speak to householders to explain why they should purchase double glazing? Do we need people following ambulances to hospital to explain how the injured party could claim compensation for the accident? Do we need more people in bureaucratic offices passing bits of paper and emails to each other in order to check that everything which should be done is done? The answers are no, no, no. There are already too many people engaged in these pursuits and desperately competing with each other for the limited custom.

What some of our factories could do is to employ people to produce the small-scale equipment needed for a future when oil is too expensive and local communities are moving towards limited self-sustainability: spades, forks, rakes, wheelbarrows, water butts, alcohol-driven rotovators, and other tools needed for allotments; bicycles, cycle rickshaws, shopping carts; solar panels for electricity or water heating, small wind-generators; sewing machines for dress making; smart meters for electricity and water so that households can monitor their consumption; house insulation materials; cookers and wood-burning stoves; triple-glazed windows; and perhaps hygienic systems whereby local sewage could be used on community land as a fertiliser. Other employees would be needed to sell and to maintain and repair these goods.

Why some of our arms manufacturers can't re-employ their workforces in this kind of manufacture was an issue I raised in the following letter in the *Guardian* on 30 September 2011:

Swords into Ploughshares

'It is hard to see how people can be paid to build jets that no one wants' as your editorial ('Bad news from BAE', 28 September) puts it. Agreed. But can't the BAE workforce be redirected into tackling the coming crises of energy and environment?

In the past arms manufacturers could change fast. A google search tells that on 12 April 1939 an order was placed with Vickers Armstrong at Castle Bromwich for 1000 Spitfires. Although they were aeroplane manufacturers a problem was caused by the Spitfire's advanced design, particularly the elliptical wing, which necessitated radical new production techniques to be introduced by subcontractors who were inexperienced. Nevertheless by 21 July 1941 all had been delivered. Over the next five years comparable orders were delivered in around 18 months and by the end of the war over 11,000 had been built.

The driving force was the need to defend the country against a powerful threat. Today there are the powerful threats of peak oil and climate change. Why can't BAE, instead of sacking 3,000 workers, redirect their manufacturing skills into smart meters, solar panels, wind turbines, wave generators, house insulating materials, rickshaws, bicycles, and other products needed to make the country self-reliant in energy. Judging by his conference speech, if Ed Miliband were prime minister this would happen.

But overall there will not be many such jobs – and they already face stiff international competition. It may be necessary to raise tariffs to protect such home-based industries from overseas competition – and that has serious ramifications in terms of the free trade requirements of the European Union. But since oil peaking and global warming are threats not just to Britain but to the whole world, we can expect that other industrialised countries will find it imperative to do likewise and will reconstruct their economies on principles of national self-sufficiency.

Yes, our economists need to rethink their fundamental tenets and come to recognise that economic growth and the global trading of goods that can be produced locally (i.e. not bananas or coffee) were features of an adolescent world and not a mature adult one!

To return to the key issue, the national problem of work is that there are too few unfilled jobs, even fewer unfilled *worthwhile* jobs and virtually no prospect, however ambitious today's political parties may claim to be, of creating sufficient paid jobs for *all* the working-age people in this country. The government cannot afford to swell the ranks of the public sector by taking on the unemployed; private enterprises cannot employ many of them at a time of economic flatlining; and the opportunities for self-employment are limited and highly competitive – we do not need more decorators, window cleaners, gardeners or odd-job people.

So, what could happen? Going back to first principles, we may ask: What is work? What might it be?

What is Work ?

Wealthist Views of Work

In a society where wealth creation is the main motive for work, it is the convention to pretend that one dislikes work. 'Thank God it's Friday' is announced in many households as a preliminary to the 'holiday' of the weekend. Yet some people work harder over the weekend, both physically and mentally, than they do during the week – decorating their homes, gardening, engaging in sport and pursuing leisure interests. In keeping with the prevailing ethos of deploring the need to work, people say, and others applaud them when they do, 'When I win the National Lottery, I'll stop work and put my feet up'.

Life is divided into work and play; play is desirable, work

undesirable. 'Roll on five o'clock, when we stop work and go home.' It is certainly true that work can be monotonous and soul-destroying – but need it be?

Many jobs in factories and in offices are repetitive and tedious, and not only give no chance for people to develop their talents, but are organised to give only minimum opportunities for them to interact other than for work purposes.

Work is seen as the means of providing the necessities of life. A wealthist society inevitably separates work from play because of its emphasis on production and consumption. Work produces, play consumes – and, to most people, this is how the world goes round. It is only in the senior positions in industry and commerce that the idea of work being expressive and self-rewarding applies. The captains of industry, the designers, the scientists and the managers have opportunities to develop their talents and to relate extensively to their fellows in terms of their work tasks, and so have a commitment which results in blurring the distinction between work and play. For them work has more satisfaction than for the operatives working in the factories and offices which they control and, in the logic which is self-evident to the wealthists, the foot soldiers, with the boring jobs, are paid less for their work.

Can Work Fulfil a Deep Urge Within Ourselves?

Ferdynand Zweig, in his classic study *The British Worker* (1952),[62] expressed his findings about attitudes to work in these words:

> My worker friends often discussed with me whether a man works because he is compelled to by the necessity to make a living, or whether he works because work itself fulfils a deep urge in him, satisfies his desire for self-expression and self-assertion, and gives him a sense of dignity and self-esteem, as having a share in the

> community life. These discussions never had an entirely conclusive outcome. Most were inclined to think that the first proposition was truer to life, or that it was true of themselves; but they did not deny that the second would be true if they had to choose between work and total idleness. . . . Perhaps most men believe that the function of a job, even an interesting job, is primarily to provide money for the comforts, amenities and pleasures of life. (pp. 97–98)

To what extent can work provide opportunities for an individual to develop personal talents? It is easy to see how an architect, a cook, a designer, a nurse, a teacher, a lawyer, or a manager can develop personal talents through work, but it is less easy to see how a factory operative working at a routine task can do the same. Perhaps the fault lies in the nature of the work. While the wealthist manager designs work situations and allocates the workforce in ways which are calculated to maximise the creation of wealth, perhaps the convivialist manager of the future will make these same decisions with an eye to the opportunities that the work provides for individuals to express themselves and to make a unique contribution to the work. Certainly it is not easy to see how this can be done in present-day factories, but it is likely that in post-industrial society there will be far fewer factories, because of a reduced demand for mass-produced goods, and if these factories become mainly automated with robotic devices, there will be fewer repetitive tasks for human operatives (but more workers unemployed).

To what extent can work provide opportunities for individuals to relate to their fellows? The wealthist manager is likely to see such opportunities as reducing output because the yardstick of success is production. The manager sets out to limit opportunities for workers to relate to their fellows during work hours because this is a distraction which reduces the amount of work done. There are, of course, exceptions, such as factories where workers are organised in interacting teams with a manufacturing task which depends upon cooperation between the members of the team. Nevertheless, most managers tend to see interaction between members of the workforce as 'play' rather than 'work', and hence tend to see opportunities for interaction as consisting of the provision of tea breaks and, in 'enlightened' companies, subsidised canteens and some leisure facilities.

Schools reflect the values of society at large and so tend to distinguish between work and play – as is shown by terms such as 'playtime', 'homework', 'playground'. The idea that play is desirable and work undesirable is sometimes fostered by injunctions such as, 'If you are naughty you will stay in at playtime' and 'Unless you behave you will be given extra work to do.' Before schools became regimented by the National Curriculum and other government demands, some primary teachers required their children to 'work' in the morning, at mathematics, reading and writing, and allowed them to 'play' in the afternoon with creative and constructional materials – as long as the children had finished their 'work'.

Convivialist Views of Work

Other teachers treated all learning activities as an integration of work and play and, provided that their pupils engaged in each of the curriculum activities at some time during the day, were not concerned when these activities happened. I see this latter group of teachers as convivialists, not only because of their ubiquitous view of work, but because they put emphasis on the children deciding for themselves when they were going to engage in different activities, thus training them to be autonomous.

It seems that teachers, poets and visionaries may have better answers to the problems of work than economists.

The Lebanese poet Kahlil Gibran wrote in *The Prophet* (1926)[63] of work in terms which are convivial:

> Always you have been told that work is a curse and labour a misfortune.
> But … in keeping yourself with labour you are in truth loving life,
> And to love life through labour is to be intimate with life's inmost secret …
> And what is it to work with love?
> It is to weave the cloth with threads drawn from your heart,
> Even as if your beloved were to wear that cloth.
> It is to build a house with affection,
> Even as if your beloved were to dwell in that house.
> It is to sow seeds with tenderness and reap the harvest with joy,
> Even as if your beloved were to eat the fruit.
> It is to charge all things you fashion with a breath of your own spirit …
> Work is love made visible.
> And if you cannot work with love but only with distaste,
> It is better that you should leave your work
> And sit at the gate of the temple
> And take alms of those who work with joy.
> For if you bake bread with indifference,
> You bake a bitter bread that feeds but half man's hunger.
> And if you grudge the crushing of the grapes,
> Your grudge distils a poison in the wine. (pp. 32–35)

In an essay entitled 'Buddhist Economics' the visionary (although an economist by profession) E.F. Schumacher[64] examined the contrasting views of work which might be taken by a western economist and by a Buddhist economist. He started from the position of universal agreement that human labour is a fundamental source of wealth, but found that there is little agreement beyond:

> The modern economist has been brought up to consider 'labour' or work as little more than a necessary evil. From the point of view of the workman, it is a 'disutility'; to work is to make a sacrifice of one's leisure and comfort, and wages are a kind of compensation for the sacrifice. Hence the ideal from the point of view of the employer is to

> have output without employees, and the ideal from the point of view of the employee is to have income without employment ...
>
> The Buddhist point of view takes the function of work to be at least threefold: to give a man a chance to utilise and develop his faculties; to enable him to overcome his ego-centredness by joining with other people in a common task; and to bring forth the goods and services needed for a becoming existence ... To organise work in such a manner that it becomes meaningless, boring, stultifying, or nerve-racking for the worker would be little short of criminal; it would indicate a greater concern with goods than with people, an evil lack of compassion and a soul-destroying degree of attachment to the most primitive side of this worldly existence. Equally, to strive for leisure as an alternative to work would be considered a complete misunderstanding of one of the basic truths of human existence, namely that work and leisure are complementary parts of the same living process and cannot be separated without destroying the joy of work and the bliss of leisure. (p. 50)

We may not embrace the reincarnation views of Buddhists, but these ideas on work do suggest a convivialist way of tackling the problem of unemployment.

Tackling the Absence of Paid Work by Creating Valuable Unpaid Work

I want to argue the case for tackling worklessness by developing communities that to some extent are self-sustaining. The argument assumes that unemployed people are in receipt of citizen's income (as described in Chapter 6).

The essential idea is to enable people who have no paid work, nor any chance of obtaining any, with the opportunity to escape the cycle implied by this story.

> A social scientist is interviewing a working man.
> Interviewer: Why do you work?
> Worker: To earn money.

Interviewer: Why do you want money?
Worker: To pay for my food and lodgings and fun.
Interviewer: Why do you want food and lodgings and fun?
Worker: So that I am fit and strong and contented.
Interviewer: Well, why do want to be these things?
Worker: So that I can work.

The audience is expected to laugh. Why? Because we have grown up in a capitalist world where work is seen as the means to the good life and not part of the good life itself.

Everybody needs money to buy the necessities of life. Most people have a job which provides this money. Some people have no job and receive money as a benefit from the state. Children depend upon the money of their parent(s). Older people depend upon pensions. That is today's model.

A different model can be imagined starting with the premise that everybody, from birth to death, receives a citizen's income from the state. This is just sufficient to live a meagre life on. Most people supplement this income with a paid job. Some cannot find a paid job but work in the programme of the local community. In families it may often be the case that one parent is in paid employment and the other engaged in unpaid community work, unpaid home-making, and unpaid child-care.

Instead of thinking on the scale of nation, county or district, I want to start with the parish. In most rural and many suburban parts of the country the local unit of government is the parish – with a parish council which, if very limited in its powers, is a democratic body elected by the local adults. Parishes vary in size from a hundred or so households to several thousand. According to Wikipedia there are 8,500 parish councils in England and they embrace 35% of the population.

Before I elaborate upon suggestions for parish sustainability, you may properly ask about the other 65% of the population, living for the most part in denser living spaces. Local government in England is gloriously complicated, with metropolitan boroughs, London boroughs, non-metropolitan districts, unitary authorities and other bodies which are exceptional in various ways. In principle, though, however naïve this may seem, they could be sub-divided into parishes for the purposes which I shall describe. There is, I admit, the considerable problem of drawing boundaries to delineate parishes, but it could be done.

Parishes as Self-Sustaining Communities Sub-divided into Manors

The basic idea is that parishes could become to some extent self-sustaining – that is, they could look after themselves by growing some of the food they need, generating some of the energy they consume, and in some ways caring for the disabled, infirm and aged of the parish. Essentially this needs to be done on a very local scale.

Suppose that a particular parish council votes to participate in a Community Self-Sustaining (CSS) programme. Suppose that this means that for, say, five years they will have an 'executive mayor' who is a trained professional worker who will work full time leading the CSS development of the parish. He or she will be chosen by the parish council as someone they feel they can trust and someone they believe can help their parish. This executive mayor will be paid for by the national government for the five years of office and will have a limited sum available each year for parish projects.

The first task for the executive mayor will be a geographical one – of dividing the parish into what we may call 'manors', each an area with between, say, ten and fifty households. These manors are going to be the main agencies for the CSS programme. Inevitably, those in some manors will be eager to participate and others will reject the idea – so the mayor works with those whose inhabitants choose to participate. The workforce of the manor will be the unemployed and retired people who choose to take part and are able to do so. The manor must be small enough for people to know each other and learn to trust each other, but large enough to have sufficient people to undertake whatever tasks are chosen for it by the manor.

The executive mayor will then seek to identify persons who can take the lead, as a voluntary task, of developing the CSS programme in each manor. Since 'manor' is a medieval term, let's use another such term for this volunteer – 'reeve'.

Manors and Reeves: a twenty-first-century version of medieval community management

The first task of the reeve is to foster any sense of neighbourliness that exists in the manor, or, if it is lacking, to begin to try to create it. Neighbourliness is having positive answers to questions like these:

- Do you know the people in the houses near to you?
- Do you ever visit each other's houses?
- If you ran out of, say, milk, would you ask a neighbour for some?
- If you are away would they put out your refuse bin and take it in when emptied?
- If you were to fall ill would you expect anyone nearby to come and support you?
- When a new family moves into the neighbourhood are they welcomed?

These are, in a way, very intimate questions about a neighbourhood. In some places such relationships are taken for granted, in others, sadly, they are not.

One way that the reeve could begin this process is through the Big Lunch. This is a national programme of street parties, all held on the same summer day and promoted by the Eden Centre in Cornwall. This remarkable process, started in 2008, has been picked up by small communities all over Britain. The national government has no part in it at all – it is just a happy idea promoted by a few entrepreneurs – and with no money changing hands! It is described as:

> a day when, for a few glorious hours, cars stop, shyness stops, gloom stops and Britain comes together in the street to meet, greet, share, swap, sing, play, and laugh for no reason other than we all need to.

The second task for the reeve will be to conduct some kind of a survey and census of the manor. She/he will need to learn which people could be involved one way or another in the CSS programme. Who are unemployed and could become active in the project? Who are elderly or infirm and may benefit from local support and help? Who live under roofs that could carry solar energy panels? Is there unused land that could be turned into allotments?

The overall aim of the CSS programme should be to develop some sustainability in each manor. To this end, there could be three major objectives for the manor to try to work towards:

1. Growing food;
2. Generating energy;
3. Supporting members of the manor who are sick, infirm or otherwise in need of help.

For growing potatoes, other vegetables and fruit, the manor needs some land which can be treated as common land. It might be a communal plot or land divided into individual allotments. Chickens might be reared for eggs and for meat. This is going to be easier in rural and suburban areas. It may be that only the third objective can be achieved in densely populated urban areas – unless roofs can house both vegetable plots and solar panels.

The most obvious way of generating energy is solar panels on roofs – for either hot water or electricity. In some areas small wind turbines may be appropriate, and where there is sufficient common land quick-growing wood, such as pollarded willows, could provide fuel for wood-burning stoves.

Supporting those in need of help will depend upon the extent to which neighbourliness has developed. For the infirm elderly such help could be a vital aid to enable them to stay in their own homes.

An important aspect of the concept of the manor is that it is small enough to act as an everybody-participating democracy. Decisions on what to grow and how to share what has been grown should be taken by the manor as a whole, acting under the leadership of the reeve. This will all be part of the growth of local neighbourliness.

It is not intended that anywhere should be completely self-contained; rather, the idea is that people should find *some* alternatives to buying everything with money obtained in employment and from citizen's income. And for those who have the capacity to be productive but are workless – either because there are no jobs, or because they have retired but still have some energy – these voluntary activities could add the mystical quality of meaning to their lives as well as providing opportunities for them to associate with others in undertaking worthwhile tasks. As noted earlier, they would all need some state income – citizen's income – which, of course, comes from the taxes paid by those across the country in paid work.*

* There is a coherence between the ideas of citizen's income, minimum and maximum wage, and community self-sustainability, but it could lead to large numbers of people choosing unpaid community work rather than paid but uncongenial employment, and clearly this could affect the revenue from taxation. This eventuality would require careful planning by the Treasury to make the system work.

The executive mayor would be an adviser to the reeves and also the source of limited funds allocated by government for the purchase of tools, seeds, energy-generating equipment, and so on. She/he would negotiate payments to be made by the electricity companies for any electricity put into the national grid by the contributing manors in the parish. She/he might establish a parish 'food market' once a week where any surplus from the manor allotments could be sold – or bartered. In addition, the mayor might organise – or cause to be organised – sports and social events for the parish.

These suggestions do not mean that provision by the manor is intended to totally supplant national provision. In particular, the work of the social services and the National Health Service would not be reduced, but would be augmented by the local volunteering. But our present dependence on imported foods and fuels would be reduced, and this would prepare us all for any major crises that might lie ahead.

Over time, other forms of self-sufficiency might develop. For example, eco-houses might be constructed and simple furniture made. Also, existing clubs, sports facilities and local societies might become involved and new ones might develop in accord with local interests.

After five years, say, the executive mayor should be replaced by a democratically elected mayor of the parish – a local person who, to the best of their ability, would continue the sustainable development of the parish and its manors.

Does this all sound like the probably phony idyll of Merrie England before land enclosures robbed the peasantry of the opportunity of growing their own crops? It is not. It is an answer to the enforced idleness that rampant forms of capitalism put undeservedly onto some communities. It is an answer to the loss of paid employment that may arise as the national economy flatlines. It is an answer to peak oil, in so far as transport will become more difficult and people will need to live more within their own communities. It is an answer to the damage that may be done by the freak storms associated with global warming, because communities will be more geared to supporting each other.

With the benefit of scientific understanding of small-scale agriculture and small-scale energy generation, it can herald worthwhile activity for the workless of today. By mobilising volunteers, it can foster community support for the aged and infirm by helping them to live in their own homes.

Above all, it can put meaning into the lives of people who have little prospect of paid employment but every opportunity for community involvement.

I finished writing the first draft of this chapter in July 2011 with these words:

> Doubtless this is naïvely expressed. But I believe there is a nugget of gold, a glimmer of hope, in these ideas.

Transition Towns: a response to a future of peak oil and climate change

A week later I came across Rob Hopkins' book *The Transition Handbook: from oil dependency to local resilience*,[65] which had been first published three years earlier. He wrote:

> Central to this book is the concept of resilience – familiar to ecologists, but less so to the rest of us. Resilience refers to the ability of a system, from individual people to whole economies, to hold together and maintain their function in the face of change and shocks from the outside. (p. 12)

And what were 'the shocks from the outside' that he was concerned about? Peak oil and climate change. As on other occasions, I found someone had already written about concerns that I had felt lonely with.

> The *Transition Handbook* is more than just a book of problems and ideas. It is about solutions, and about the Transition model, which I think may turn out to be the foundation for one of the most important social, political and cultural movements of the 21st century. . . .
>
> Rebuilding local agriculture and food production, localising energy production, rethinking healthcare, rediscovering local building materials in the context of zero energy building, rethinking how we manage waste, all build resilience and offer the potential of an extraordinary renaissance – economic, cultural and spiritual;. I am not afraid of a world with less consumerism, less 'stuff' and no economic growth. Indeed I am more frightened of the opposite. (pp. 14–15)

Having studied *The Transition Handbook*, I realise that my ideas on neighbourliness, care for the elderly, sick and infirm, solar panels on roofs, allotments, etc. are in step with what Hopkins has been developing.

I think they are in tune with the democratic theory that government should not be the fiefdom of the rich and powerful but a manifestation of the will of the people. Parochial manors with competent reeves may be an important answer to unemployment today and to many of the problems of the future.

8

Rethinking Energy without Fossil or Nuclear Fuel

Keep the home fires burning . . .
There's a silver lining,
Through the dark clouds shining.
Turn the dark cloud inside out . . .

—Lena Gilbert Ford (1914)

Chapter 2 discussed the inevitable fact that demand for global supplies of oil will soon exceed supply – that is, peak oil will soon occur – and indeed, this may already be happening. Oil wells across the world are being pumped dry, and although geologists identify substantial oil deposits under the Arctic and elsewhere, the hazards to oil men and to the environment, the high costs of extraction, and the gigantic costs of cleaning up in the Arctic waters if there are spills are powerful arguments for not trying to tap them.

As it becomes scarcer, the price of oil as a chemical raw material, as a heating fuel and, when refined, as petrol will steadily rise, with profound effects on the goods for sale in our shops, our ability to heat our homes and our opportunities for driving our own cars.

What action should government take?

Energy Consumption in the UK in 2010

The UK is hugely dependent on fossil fuels – coal, oil and gas – for its energy and, as is widely recognised scientifically but ignored by consumers, these all liberate carbon dioxide which, through the greenhouse effect, is causing global warming. Since the 1980s coal burning has become minimal, but oil and gas burning is ubiquitous.

Before considering ways of reducing this consumption, it is useful to survey the energy structure of the UK. Data published in July 2011 by the Department of Energy and Climate Change[66] have enabled me to put together the following account. The unit of energy is known as the 'tonne of oil equivalent' and, of course, this is measured in millions.

The following figures are all based on what is called 'final energy consumption', which means the point at which fuels and electrical energy are being used to warm homes, power domestic equipment and lights, drive machinery, etc., or be converted into products.*

For 2010, the final energy consumption of the UK was measured by the Department of Energy and Climate Change as being 150.1 million tonnes of oil equivalent. Electricity and gas are measured in terms of the amount of oil that would generate an equivalent amount of energy.

Yes, I agree: one doesn't feel much the wiser, not even when thinking of it as 2.4 tonnes of oil equivalent for every man, woman and child in 2010 in the UK – which is slightly more than a domestic oil tank holds for oil-fired central heating. But when

* 'Final energy consumption' is less than 'primary energy consumption', which refers to energy in terms of fuels in the form obtained directly from natural sources. For example, for solid fuels, while the primary energy consumption in 2010 was 15% of the total, the final energy consumption was 2%. Most of the primary consumption was spent on generating electricity.

we look at this in terms of different types of energy source and different uses, it becomes more meaningful.

Final Energy Consumption in the UK: the five sources

In 2010, the energy consumed in the UK came from five sources:

Oil*	43%
Natural gas	34%
Electricity	19%
Renewable fuels	2%
Solid fuels	2%
Total	*100%*

But what is the origin of these sources?

Oil is complicated because some is imported refined, some is imported crude and refined here, and some is exported. However, in 2010, roughly 25% of our oil consumption was from offshore UK oil wells, and 75% from other countries (two thirds from Norway and only a seventh from OPEC countries).

Natural gas from the North Sea beds began to be piped across the UK from 1967, and for 40 years was a major source of energy. Gas is used domestically, and for the generation of electricity when coal-fired power stations are converted or replaced by gas-fired ones. But by the mid-2000s our supplies were reducing and we began to import natural gas – through pipelines across the North Sea – from Belgium, the Netherlands and Norway, and by shipments of LNG (liquefied natural gas) from a number of Middle East countries. In 2010, just under half of our natural gas was imported, and there have been recurrent

* The term 'oil' is used here to describe the whole range of liquid fossil fuels, including petrol, diesel, heating oil, etc.

fears that Russia, which provides much of the gas that flows across Europe, could threaten this supply in a new version of the old cold war.

Recently the UK gas industry has seen new hope in what is called shale gas. The United States has been recovering shale gas for some time in Texas and other parts of the country. Recently, preliminary wells drilled in Lancashire around Blackpool have found substantial reserves which the company concerned claim could replace the declining indigenous gas supplies from the UK North Sea wells. The process for getting this gas involves hydraulic fracturing of underground shale rocks ('fracking') by pumping down, under high pressure, water, sand and chemicals, which opens fissures that enable the gas to flow into the well. But environmentalists are worried because of fears that water aquifers, supplying domestic water, could be seriously contaminated. For this reason, fracking has been banned in some parts of the United States, France and Germany. Environmentalists are also concerned that financial investment that might otherwise go into wind farms (in which there is no production of greenhouse gases) may instead be diverted into shale gas (which, when burned, releases carbon dioxide into the atmosphere).

The supply of **electricity** in 2010 in the UK came from a variety of sources – namely: natural gas, 40%; coal, 32%; nuclear, 17%; other fuels, 8%; wind and wave power, 1%; hydro, less than 1%; and imports, 1%.

Renewable fuels are wood and wood waste burned on domestic fires, and liquid biofuels (mainly imported) used in vehicles.

Nearly 60% of solid fuels (coal) is imported, and nearly all is consumed in coal-fired power stations.

Oil, gas, coal and fuel wood can be stored, but electricity can't – save for limited amounts in batteries – and its 'renewable' sources are variable; thus, wind power depends upon wind blowing (the offshore wind turbines get sufficient wind to turn all the time, but onshore ones are not always turning); hydro-electric power depends upon rainfall (but usually this is adequate); and solar power (very limited as yet in the UK) depends on the sun shining and so, necessarily is a daytime source.

Nuclear power is seen by the government as the main source of electricity in the future (at present providing 17%), but produces radioactive wastes, some of which (in terms of today's technology) will have to be safeguarded in cooled stores for several hundred years – an awful legacy for the future.

Energy Consumption for Transport, Domestic Uses, Industry and Services

And where is the energy consumed? The following list shows how our energy consumption is shared by four sectors:

Transport	38%
Domestic	32%
Industry	18%
Services	12%
Total	*100%*

These sectors are later sub-divided into different users, when consideration is given to how our energy consumption can be reduced.

Consequences of Oil Supply Diminishing

It is clear from this analysis that as global oil production peaks, leading to diminishing supplies and steady increases in its cost, the effect on the UK economy will be devastating. It may be that oil mined in the Arctic and off the coast of Shetland will keep the petrol pumps going, but the cost will be high because of the difficulty of working on the sea bottom. Likewise, tar sands may provide oil at a price, and other sources may be discovered and exploited. But it will only delay by a few years the crunch fact that the source of energy for virtually all of our transport – oil – is running out.

While global natural gas supplies, largely from Russian gas fields, seem to have adequate reserves for some time, global politics could lead to sudden shortages as our own supplies from the North Sea become exhausted. It may be that Lancashire shale gas will replace what comes from the North Sea gas wells, but that depends upon the success and acceptance of the fracking technology. Recent minor earth tremors in Lancashire have not helped to allay fears about the safety of this procedure.

Some suggest that electricity will take the place of oil as an energy source, and that most of this can come from nuclear power stations. We will look at this possibility shortly, but first it will be helpful to focus on the steps being taken in the UK to reduce our carbon footprint by cutting back on our emissions of greenhouse gases.

Climate Change Act 2008

In October 2008 the Labour government committed the UK to cutting greenhouse gas emissions by 80% of their 1990 levels by 2050.[67] This was the first public move of Ed Miliband, Secretary of State in the just formed Department for Energy and Climate Change, and it was supported by his Conservative opposite number in Parliament. It was based on the recommendations of the Parliamentary Climate Change Committee chaired by Lord Adair Turner. It is noteworthy that this committee consisted of economists, scientists and climate change experts.

This was an epoch-making decision that would substantially reduce the continuing increase in global temperature and the associated climate change – if, but only if, the other industrial nations of the world would do the same.

The report[68] of the Parliamentary Climate Change Committee of December 2008 notes that it had advised the government on 7 October 2008 that:

- The UK should aim to reduce Kyoto greenhouse gas emissions by at least 80% below 1990 levels by 2050 (77% below 2005 levels). This would be an appropriate UK contribution to a global deal aiming to reduce Kyoto greenhouse gas emissions to between 20–24 billion tonnes by 2050 (about 50–60% below current global levels).
- The 80% target should apply to the sum of all sectors of the UK economy, including international aviation and shipping. To the extent that international aviation and shipping emissions are not reduced by 80%, more effort would have to be made in other sectors.
- The costs to the UK from this level of emissions reduction can be made affordable – we estimate between 1–2% of GDP in 2050 – with appropriate policies and given early action to put the UK on an appropriate path. Our estimates are the same order of magnitude as those provided by the Stern Review and other global and UK studies.

This was immediately written into the Climate Change Bill and put to Parliament later in October 2008; it became law in December.

The first two paragraphs of the Climate Change Act say:

(1) It is the duty of the Secretary of State to ensure that the net UK carbon account for the year 2050 is at least 80% lower than the 1990 baseline.

(2) 'The 1990 baseline' means the aggregate amount of:
   (a) net UK emissions of carbon dioxide for that year, and
   (b) net UK emissions of each of the other targeted greenhouse gases for the year that is the base year for that gas.

To cut to 80% of the 1990 baseline in 40 years means a reduction year by year of 2–3%.

UK Emissions of Carbon Dioxide

Figure 6* shows how the UK emissions of carbon dioxide have been decreasing since 1990, but this is largely attributable to a switch from coal-fired power stations to gas-fired, which, while still pumping carbon dioxide into the atmosphere, put out less per unit of energy produced. But was the fall in 2009 due to the new act? Apparently not, for the Third Report of the Climate Change Committee (published on 30 June 2011) notes:

> The fall in emissions of almost 9% in 2009 was largely due to the recession. . . . Economy-wide emissions increased by 2.9% in 2010. However, without the impacts of the cold weather, emissions would have been broadly flat.[69]

The 225 pages of this report are packed with detailed discussion and proposals for reducing emissions, and attempt to be optimistic and positive, but the 'Key Findings' section includes this bald statement:

> Meeting carbon budgets requires an acceleration in the rate of emissions reduction.

It doesn't look very promising! Figure 7 shows what a very long way there is to go to reach the 80% reduction target for 2050.

Widespread public understanding of the gravity of the current situation is needed in order to support the necessarily strong government that can look for and implement creative ideas on how to achieve this goal.

---

* Redrawn from the above report.

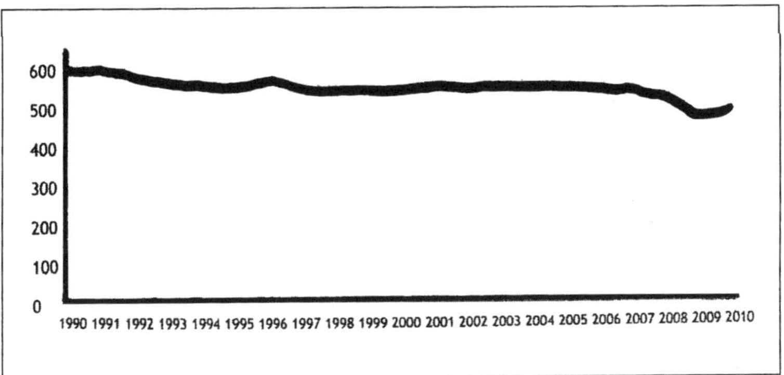

Figure 6. UK Emissions of CO_2, 1990–2010

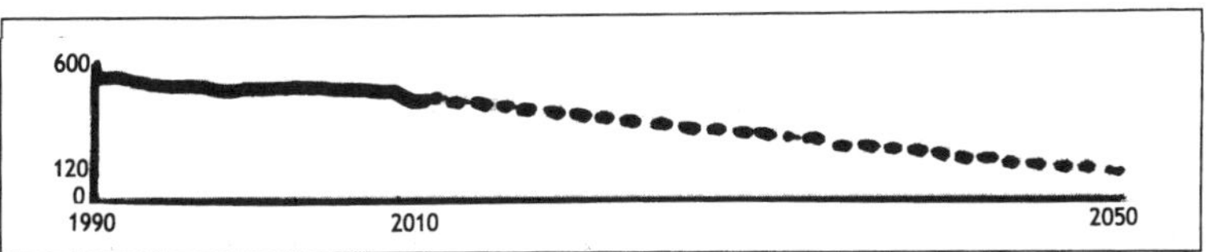

Figure 7. UK Emissions of CO_2, 1990–2050 ***(showing the reduction needed if the target is to be achieved of 80% reduction of 1990 levels {120 mt CO_2})***

Government Policy 2011

Overarching National Policy Statement for Energy

In July 2011 the UK government published an *Overarching National Policy Statement for Energy*:[70]

> We are committed to meeting our legally binding target to cut greenhouse gas emissions by at least 80% by 2050, compared to 1990 levels. Analysis done on possible 2050 pathways shows that moving to a secure, low carbon energy system is challenging, but achievable. It requires major investment in new technologies to

> renovate our buildings, the electrification of much of our heating, industry and transport, prioritisation of sustainable bio-energy and cleaner power generation. And it requires major changes in the way energy is used by individuals, by industry, and by the public sector. (Para. 2.2.1)

So far, so good. But the next paragraph shows that, in keeping with the right-wing policies of our 2011 government, it will not be the state that will make this 'major investment'; rather, private companies will be expected to do it within 'a market-based system':

> Delivering this change is a major challenge not least for energy providers, and the Government is working to ensure their efforts produce the major, rapid change the UK needs. Within a market-based system and with severe constraints on public expenditure in the near-term, the focus of Government activity in this transformation is clear. It should be on developing a clear, long-term policy framework which facilitates investment in the necessary new infrastructure (by the private sector) and in energy efficiency. (Para. 2.2.2)

The intention is to replace, as far as possible, fossil-fuel sources of energy with electricity generated by nuclear power, wind power and – hopefully – coal-burning stations where the carbon dioxide produced is captured. (The technology for the latter has yet to be developed effectively.)

Chancellor of the Exchequer: 'not going to save the planet …'

Whether the above statements of government policy were realistic in terms of the coming crises of global warming and peak oil is doubtful, but George Osborne, Chancellor of the Exchequer, shattered hopes with his Autumn Forecast Statement in November 2011:

> I am worried about the combined impact of the green policies adopted not just in Britain, but also by the European Union, on

> some of our heavy, energy-intensive industries. We are not going to save the planet by shutting down our steel mills, aluminium smelters and paper manufacturers.... If we burden them with endless social and environmental goals – however worthy in their own right – then not only will we not achieve those goals, but the businesses will fail, jobs will be lost, and our country will be poorer.[71]

Many environmentalists paraphrased this speech as 'we are not going to save the planet – full stop'.

The Promise (or Worry) of Nuclear Energy

The first UK nuclear power station (Calder Hall) began putting electricity into the grid in 1956, and by 1997 a quarter of our electricity came from nuclear power. But since then a number of nuclear power stations have come to the end of their working life and have closed, so that by 2009 only about a sixth of UK electricity was nuclear in origin.[72]

Worries about a future 'energy gap' led to the government conducting a nationwide consultation on nuclear power in 2007; the outcome was to give the go-ahead for more stations to be built, and eight sites in England and Wales have been designated as suitable for commercial development. The Scottish government has rejected nuclear power.

This is the introduction to the statement on nuclear power in the government's *Overarching National Policy Statement for Energy* (July 2011):[73]

> For the UK to meet its energy and climate change objectives, the Government believes that there is an urgent need for new electricity generation plant, including new nuclear power. Nuclear power generation is a low carbon, proven technology, which is anticipated to play an increasingly important role as we move to diversify and decarbonise our sources of electricity.

It is Government policy that new nuclear power should be able to contribute as much as possible to the UK's need for new capacity. (Paras 3.5.1 and 3.5.2)

Objections to Nuclear Power

Environmental groups such as Greenpeace and Friends of the Earth campaign against the further deployment of nuclear power. Objections include the worldwide concern that some states could use their nuclear energy facilities to manufacture nuclear weapons; the fear that terrorists could take over a power station and use the threat of releasing radioactivity as a form of blackmail; the possibility of human error causing a massive discharge of radioactive material into the atmosphere (as happened at Chernobyl in 1986); and the possibility of earthquakes or tsunami waves damaging a plant and releasing toxicity (as happened at Fukushami in 2010). But the major reason that I, in company with many others, reject it is that, to date, there is no effective way of safely disposing of high-level radioactive waste. All we can do is pass it from one generation to the next to safeguard.

In 2003 the UK government set up the Committee on Radioactive Waste Management (CoRWM)[74] – an independent body to advise on the long-term management of radioactive wastes. In July 2006 it recommended that geological disposal is the best available long-term solution, and that in the meantime safe and secure interim storage is needed.

Plutonium is probably the most dangerous radioactive material under consideration. CoRWM reported in 2009:

> When all the fuel in the current UK power programme has been reprocessed there will be about 100 tonnes of separated civil plutonium that requires long-term management. Most of the existing separated plutonium is in store at Sellafield, plus a small amount of (about 2 tonnes) at Dounreay. Continued storage of plutonium is not a viable option in the long term for various reasons, including that it

> is expensive and has the potential to give rise to considerable worker doses.[75]

So, what should be done with it? CoRWM recommends continued storage until 2120, then immobilising the plutonium in a suitable waste form and disposing of the waste in a geological facility.

Yes. Keep it carefully for the next 110 years and then expect our great-great-great grandchildren to drop it into a deep hole in the ground. Unbelievable. Greenpeace commented:

> This is an environmental time bomb for future generations because the waste will inevitably degrade and leak.

Until the problem of how to dispose safely – for ever – of radioactive wastes from nuclear power stations has been solved, we should not allow any more such power stations to be built.

Nuclear Policies Around the World

The UK government seems out of step with a number of other European countries. Following the accident in Japan, Germany decided in May 2011 to phase out nuclear power and to close all reactors by 2022. Belgium is planning a similar shutdown. In France the socialists will shut down nearly half of the country's reactors if they win the forthcoming presidential election. In Italy in June 2011, a national referendum cancelled the building of all new reactors. Spain is engaged in a political tussle over the present ruling party's election pledge in 2008 to phase out nuclear power. In the United States public opinion seems to be growing against nuclear power.

Wikipedia's article on nuclear energy policy gives this summary:

> Thirty-one countries operate nuclear power stations, and there are a considerable number of new reactors being built in China, South

Korea, India, and Russia. As of June 2011, countries such as Australia, Austria, Denmark, Greece, Ireland, Latvia, Liechtenstein, Luxembourg, Malta, Portugal, Israel, Malaysia, New Zealand, and Norway remain opposed to nuclear power.

The Inevitable Need to Reduce Our Consumption of Energy

Only a childless global-warming denier can say, 'There is no problem – we should continue with business as usual.' For everybody else, it must be clear that our consumption of energy has to be reduced, but at the same time most will say, 'Not yet – we need to climb out of our economic difficulties first.'

They are wrong. It is on the issue of changing and reducing our energy consumption that the three problems of a struggling economy, the peaking of oil and global warming converge and need to be tackled together.

The economic growth of nations like ours has required a greedy consumption of fossil fuel, and the resultant carbon dioxide is warming the earth and causing massive climate change. Hence, a reduction in oil consumption (due to substantial price increases as production falls when the oil fields begin to dry up) will reduce the global carbon footprint and so hopefully eventually reduce the increases in global temperature. But a reduction in oil consumption will also require a massive restructuring of the economies of industrial countries like the UK. It is inevitable. Unless we restructure, such a reduction will slowly cause massive dislocation of our economy and heavy job losses.

Reduce Our Economy

Suppose that, instead of seeking economic growth, the UK set out on a deliberate policy of economic cutback, with a clear commitment to improve the quality of life for everybody.

That is such a momentous statement that it needs repeating:

Suppose that instead of seeking economic growth, the UK set out on a deliberate policy of economic cutback, with a clear commitment to improve the quality of life for everybody.

Provided the citizen's income, minimum living wage and maximum take-home wage discussed in Chapter 6 are in place, and communities are beginning to develop by recognising the power of unpaid work, as set out in Chapter 7, it could happen.

Kick Start: a four-day week with 80% wage for above-average earners

One way of kick-starting such a policy would be to cut the working week. Suppose, for example, that every company or public body with more than 100 employees was required, by statute, to cut the working week to four days for everyone who is paid above the current median average wage (at present, £25,900 per year). Yes, these people would take a salary cut of 20% too – but they would have the pleasure of a three-day weekend. Where a company insists that their business requires the full week for such employees, heavy taxation might be imposed.

Alternatively, these people might work a five-day week for four months and then have a month off.

Unfair on the lower paid who still have to work five days? Yes – but they need the income that comes from the wages of those five days.

The economic result would be that many of the better-off people would be less able to afford the luxuries that they have hitherto enjoyed, and so the section of our economy producing these luxury goods would be reduced.

Reduce Our Use of Fuel for Transport

The transport sector used 55.7 million tonnes of oil equivalent in 2010, which equalled 38% of UK final energy consumption. Of this, 50% went on passenger cars, 23% on road freight, 22% on air travel, 3% on water transport and 2% on railways. Nearly 100% of transport ran on oil.

Personal Transport: passenger cars

While car manufacturers' efforts to make their vehicles more efficient and run more miles per litre are laudable, it might be better if they began to look for simpler forms of personal transport. Electric cars are beginning to become available, and storage batteries are improving, but at a price to the purchaser – and at a price to the world too, because the electricity has to be made, and if it comes from nuclear energy there are the future risks associated with storage of high-level radioactive wastes.

If people become more focused on their local community (as suggested in Chapter 7), the bicycle, tricycle, tandem, and bicycle rickshaw will become the common personal means of transport, along with walking. The transition will be harsh – but healthy.

Increased fuel costs will affect all car drivers – but, as is the way with an unregulated situation, the rich will continue to drive while the less well-off give up their cars – unless, in the face of the crisis, petrol is rationed.

Kick Start: reduce motorway speed limit

An immediate start to saving fuel would be to limit motorway speeds to 50 mph, which, scientists claim, would reduce fuel usage by 20–30%.[76]

Sadly, in September 2011 the present government proposed to raise the speed limit to 80 mph. (And it claims to be the greenest government ever!)

> Transport secretary Philip Hammond said the existing 70mph limit was 'out of date', and that Britain needed to be 'back in the fast lane of global economies'... . The analysis published by the Climate Change Committee in a report to parliament in June 2011 showed the proposed increase could add emissions of up to 2.2m tonnes CO_2/year.[77]

Kick Start: ration books for fuel

To kick-start the steady reduction of transport fuel, every car owner, on purchasing the road fund licence (for six months or a year, as now), could also be given a ration book with coupons to be given up when purchasing fuel. Recognising that some have greater travel needs than others, it is suggested that it could be permissible to trade these coupons for cash. Year by year the government could reduce the number of coupons in the ration books, thus slowly reducing the national consumption of transport fuel.

Road Freight

Similar arrangements might be used for freight transport. As the economy declines, so will the need for freight transport, and it can be envisaged that the manufacture and production of goods – from foods to furniture – will be carried out nearer to the place of purchase. It maybe that a limited production of biofuels will suffice to keep essential freight moving, but it will be important that the fields used for growing the crops which will be fermented into fuel are not taking over fields needed for growing food.

Air Travel

As the price of oil increases, the airlines will need to raise their fares. Inevitably there will be fewer people able to jet across the world for holidays. Those of the jet set who choose to work four months on and one month off, as suggested above, could at least visit anywhere in Europe using trains – which use much less fuel.

Business people might find that video conferencing is an

alternative to flying around the globe, but also, of course, there may be less demand for their services if the economy becomes more localised.

Reduce Our Domestic Energy

The domestic sector used 48.9 million tonnes of oil equivalent in 2010, which equalled 32% of UK final energy consumption. This was used for space heating (61%), water heating (18%), lighting and appliances (18%), and cooking (3%). It was supplied by natural gas (69%), electricity (21%), oil (6%), and other fuels (4%.)

Clearly our homes and places of work need to use less energy on space heating. Current policies of heat insulation are a proper course of action. But how about lowering the winter temperature of many of our buildings? Until central heating came into our homes from the 1960s on, the response to colder weather was to wear more clothes. Is it too simple to suggest that this could still happen?

Kick Start: tariffs that encourage less use of fuel, not more

One way of kick-starting this would be to have domestic fuel tariffs such that the more gas, oil or electricity used, the higher the unit price. If every household had smart meters that enabled them to watch how much energy was being consumed, this might encourage them to switch off appliances when not needed. It might mean an end to the ridiculous proliferation of energy companies touting incomprehensible tariffs, and a return to pre-Thatcher state ownership.

Generate Domestic Energy Domestically

Limited amounts of energy can be generated by households and communities themselves. Solar panels on house roofs can be used to heat domestic water (which can be stored in insulated tanks) and to generate electricity – when the sun shines. The problem is one of storage of electricity, since most domestic usage is at night. There is an urgent need for further development of the technology concerned with battery storage of electricity. But an alternative way of storing electricity from domestic solar panels would involve using it to electrolyse water and storing the hydrogen generated. This is a technological solution that also deserves urgent attention.

Wood-burning stoves can be used to heat houses, and communities might be helped to plant fast-growing wood that could be burned in them. There is some doubt as to whether household wind turbines would provide significant electricity for domestic use, but in some locations they might be appropriate.

Reduce Our Industrial Use of Energy

The industrial sector used 27.5 m tonnes oil equivalent in 2010, representing 18% of UK energy consumption. This was used by the chemicals industry (16%); the food, drink and tobacco industries (12%); vehicle, electrical and mechanical engineering industries (11%); mineral products industries (10%); textile, paper, printing and publishing industries (10%); iron and steel industries (5%); non-ferrous metals industries (2%); the construction industry (2%); and other industries (32%). It was supplied by natural gas (38%), electricity (32%), oil (18%), and other fuels (12%).

As community life grows, there will be less demand for goods from afar, and as freight becomes more expensive while the economy no longer grows, it is clear that the manufacture of goods for consumer purchase will become reduced in scale and hence the consumption of industrial energy will likewise shrink. Few today can doubt that the volume of paper pushed through our letter boxes is mostly unread and that, even if recycled, it is a waste of energy. Whether the farming industry will find ways of reducing chemical fertilisers and utilising sewage is an important question. Home and local production of food may signal an end to the large-scale manufacture of foodstuffs. On the other hand, the production of tools for local food production, of domestic equipment for self-sufficiency, of personal-transport vehicles such as bicycles and rickshaws, of wind turbines for the offshore and onshore generation of electricity, and a host of other products needed for the reconstruction of a convivial society will all require industrial energy. In particular, the chemical industry will need such limited supplies of oil as are available: to burn it will be seen as a dire waste, and the pharmaceutical industry needs to be protected in order to provide the medicines that help maintain the nation's health. Perhaps taking natural gas, oil and other fuels out of the equation, leaving the present 32% coming from electricity, will be the path taken by industry.

This all sounds naïve – but it demonstrates the kind of changes that are going to be inevitable.

Reduce the Energy use of the Service Sector

The service sector used 18.4 m tonnes oil equivalent in 2010, which was 12% of UK energy consumption. This was used by commercial firms (54%), public administration (30%), agriculture (5%), and miscellaneous enterprises (10%). It was supplied by electricity (47%), natural gas (42%), oil (10%), and other sources (1%). Excluding agriculture, 45% of this sector's energy consumption went on space heating.

The inevitable reduction in transport, as described above, will lead to the demise of supermarkets and big stores and probably to the regeneration of a few shops in every town, selling local produce and locally made goods. This is likely to make a substantial energy reduction – particularly in terms of space heating, provided that, as in domestic premises, there is ample insulation and, possibly, lower temperatures are maintained during the winter months. With the same applying in public administration offices, a further reduction can be envisaged.

What Hope is there for a Country without Fossil Fuel and Rejecting Nuclear Power?

It is a tough question. Of course, in the past, before coal came on the scene, everybody lived their lives without the energy sources that we, their descendents, have come to take for granted. But it is a question that either we, or our children in even more difficult circumstances, must answer.

We must accelerate the construction of offshore and onshore wind turbines, begin to re-orient our industries towards creating the means of self-sufficiency, plant extensive plots of fast-growing trees for wood-burners, ensure that every building where people live or work is thoroughly insulated against the cold of winter, invest heavily in domestic solar panels for hot water and for electricity, and work intelligently in all the directions suggested by ideas of sustainability, including undertaking massive research and development projects on electrical storage and hydrogen usage. As noted earlier, at a personal level there is one step that is easy: get sufficient warm clothes! It can be done. We must first, however, recognise that this is what the future will look like.

One benefit from these reductions would be that the UK's dependence on imported energy would decrease, and so the likelihood of international tension would diminish. Soon we might find that we no longer need military might to fight wars to protect our energy supplies. Instead, our military could become a force ready to defend our island if any greedy nation thought we had something worth plundering (this sounds like medieval times), and, more significantly, it would be a rapid reaction force to respond to any climatic catastrophes that occur here or anywhere in the world where humanitarian assistance is needed quickly.

Who Dares? But Who Will Endanger the Future by Doing Nothing?

It will take a brave government to implement such austere measures. But it must be said that any government that believes that such changes can be achieved merely through market forces and private investments, with a gentle nudge from government, oversees territory that can only be described as cloud-cuckoo land.

It is essential that government governs: that is why it has been elected. The changing of energy supply and consumption needs to be tightly controlled and coordinated. Of the many tasks facing future governments, that is the most central and vital.

It must be carried out with a prime concern for the quality of life of all the people, not for the opportunity it presents for a few people to profit. And great care must be taken to explain to the electorate why, in the face of the inevitable, each step is necessary.

It is worth looking at the insight, courage and incipient statesmanship of the Labour Party in 1945 as it faced up to the need to reconstruct much of the country's infrastructure after the Second World War. In its election manifesto, its leaders said that they would take 'public ownership of the fuel and power industries':

> For a quarter of a century the coal industry, producing Britain's most precious national raw material, has been floundering chaotically under the ownership of many hundreds of independent companies. Amalgamation under public ownership will bring great economies in

> operation ... Public ownership of gas and electricity undertakings will lower charges, prevent competitive waste, open the way for co-ordinated research and development, and lead to the reforming of uneconomic areas of distribution. Other industries will benefit.[78]

The next two parts of the industrial programme were to nationalise inland transport and the iron and steel industries. The manifesto added an important note of common humanity:

> These socialised industries, taken over on a basis of fair compensation, ... [will] be conducted efficiently in the interests of consumers, coupled with proper status and conditions for the workers employed in them.

Similar measures are needed today.

The alternative – of doing nothing, of business as usual, keeping the blinkers on, and hoping for the best – will lead inevitably to social chaos within a generation as the economy staggers from one bubble crisis to the next, oil rockets in price, and climatic catastrophes, associated with global warming, become more frequent.

9

Rethinking Food Supplies in the UK

We are so dependent on oil to fuel our food supplies that we are only nine meals away from anarchy.

—Baron Ewen Cameron, Chair of the Countryside Commission (1999–2004)

Oil Peaking Will Affect Food Supplies

In Chapter 2 it is explained that the writing is on the wall for the age of fossil oil. This has major implications for the production of food. Fossil oil drives farm equipment, supports the production of chemical fertilisers, fuels the transportation of food from suppliers (by land, sea and air) to shops, and from shops to homes in family cars or supermarket deliveries, and may be the energy source for processing foods in factories, and for storing it in refrigeration plants.

As oil peaks and the price escalates, it will be inevitable that food is produced near to where it is consumed. At present, by virtue of air freight, we import some of our beef from Brazil, lamb from New Zealand, carrots from South Africa, beans from Kenya, potatoes from Israel, spring onions from Thailand, tomatoes from Saudi Arabia, asparagus from Peru, apples from California, pears from the Argentine and strawberries from Spain. All of these can be produced in the UK, and soon our reliance on overseas producers will become too expensive. The UK will need to become self-sufficient in food production. More than that, communities will find it necessary to become more reliant on locally grown food. Lorries transporting foodstuffs will no longer pound up and down the motorways. Dundee cake will not be eaten far from Dundee.

How We Feed Today

In 2009 the average expenditure of UK households on food and non-alcoholic drinks was £23.86 per person per week, with an additional £8.26 on eating out and a further £5.96 on alcoholic drinks. Table 1 shows the percentage of expenditure by households on different types of food.[79]

Table 1. UK Household Expenditure on Food, 2009

How much of the average £29 per person per week went on different foods?

Food	%
Meat	22%
Fruit and vegetables	18%
Bread, flour, cereals and biscuits	16%
Milk, cheese and eggs	13%
Sugar and sweet products	11%
Fish	5%
Potatoes	5%
Other foods	10%
Total	*100%*

Where did this food come from? Measured in terms of what is termed 'farm-gate value' (i.e. money), just half of it was from UK sources. The Netherlands supplied 6%, Spain 5%, France 4%, Germany 3%, Ireland 3%, and the remaining 29% came from

185 other countries around the world.[80] Table 2 shows for a few foods how much of what we ate in 2009 (again measured in money) was produced in the UK. For example, 82% of the money spent buying meat was for meat produced in the UK, and 18% was for meat that was imported.[81]

Table 2. UK Household Consumption of Food 2009

How much of the food consumed was produced in the UK? (in terms of money)

Meat	82%
Fruit and vegetables	23%
Apples	24%
Tomatoes	33%
Flour	85%
Milk, cheese and eggs	81%
Sugar and sweet products	62%
Potatoes	94%

A different way of looking at this is in terms of the amount of food (in weight for most foods, in litres for milk, and in quantity for eggs) is given in Table 3, which gives more detail, but refers to 2005 data.[82]

Obviously the items below the line we could not grow ourselves, but our climate is such that we could produce 100% of what we consume of the items above the line. But it would mean that we had to eat fruits and salad vegetables when in season and not, as we have become increasingly used to over the last thirty years or so, throughout the year due to imports from warmer climates. National self-sufficiency in most foodstuffs will mean learning, as our ancestors did, to savour fruits and vegetables in the months when, by careful husbandry, they ripen.

Table 3. UK Household Consumption of Food 2005

How much of the food consumed was produced in the UK? (in terms of weight/quantity)

Lamb	90%
Chicken	80%
Beef	75%
Pork	55%
Fish	38%
Milk	86%
Eggs	86%
Green peas	96%
Carrots and turnips	90%
Potatoes	86%
Green beans	85%
Brassicas	82%
Cauliflower and broccoli	51%
Onions	38%
Mushrooms	34%
Strawberries	40%
Apples	27%
Plums	14%
Lettuces	44%
Cucumbers	24%
Tomatoes	9%
....	
Bananas	0%
Lemons	0%
Oranges	0%
Pineapples	0%
Rice	0%
Tea	0%
Coffee	0%

Could the UK be Self-Sufficient in Food?

As long ago as 1975 Kenneth Mellanby, in *Can Britain Feed Herself?* (1975), gave an unambiguous 'Yes' in answer to his title. He showed that by eating less meat it would be possible to provide a nutritionally balanced diet grown on home soil.

Recently, in 2008, Simon Fairlie, editor of *The Land* magazine, has re-examined this question and shown some of the changes that would be needed not only to be self-sufficient but also to farm organically – that is, without the chemical fertilisers currently employed.[83]

> The good news for supporters of organic agriculture is that Britain can feed its industrially bloated population through organic agriculture (albeit with a reduction in meat consumption). The bad news is that it takes a lot of land compared to chemical farming, not only because yields are lower, but also because more land is required to capture nitrogen through green manure or through livestock.

Of the 243 million hectares comprising the United Kingdom, just under a tenth is agricultural and forestry land. Table 4 shows Fairlie's calculations for the way this land would be needed for

Table 4. How the UK Population of 61 Million Could Be Fed Entirely From Our 22 Million Hectares of Available Land (Simon Fairlie's calculations)

	Present practice 'agribusiness' or 'chemical farming' *million hectares*	**Self-sufficient practice** 'permaculture' or 'organic farming' *million hectares*
Arable land	4.4	7.5
Pasture	6.4	5.9
Woodland	3.7	6.0
Spare land	7.6	2.8
Total	22.2	22.2

UK self-sufficiency in food in terms of (a) the present practice of chemical farming (which, of course, depends upon the availability of oil), and (b) a permaculture of organic farming (which is not dependent on oil).

This is how Fairlie describes his concept of permaculture:

> Organic livestock agriculture becomes more efficient and sustainable when it is carried out in conjunction with other traditional and permacultural management practices which are integral to a natural fertility cycle. These include: feeding livestock upon food wastes and residues; returning human sewage to productive land; dispersal of animals on mixed farms and smallholdings, rather than concentration in large farms; local slaughter and food distribution; managing animals to ensure optimum recuperation of manure; and selecting and managing livestock, especially dairy cows, to be nitrogen providers rather than nitrogen stealers.
>
> These measures demand more human labour, and more even dispersal of both livestock and humans around the country than is the case now. Effective pursuit of livestock-based organic agriculture requires a localised economy and some degree of agrarian resettlement.

He calculates that an increase in woodland to 6 million hectares could provide three-quarters of the timber and pulp that we currently import, but adds that

> . . . a sane society, without all the junk mail, newspaper supplements no one reads, tacky throwaway furniture and so on could make do with a lot less. On the other hand six million hectares of woodland, could also produce enough firewood to heat six million well-insulated family homes.

On the assumption that fossil fuels are no longer available, he allocates 10% of the arable land to biomass which could be used to produce fuel for tractors and other farm machinery – 'or else to grow feed for draught animals'.

Implications for the Farming Community

As expressed above, Simon Fairlie's proposals sound straightforward. They wouldn't be in practice. In the UK there are some 300,000 farms with an average size of 57 hectares. However, 41,000 of these farms, on two-thirds of the agricultural area, are larger than 100 hectares. In 2006 there were 152,000 full-time farmers as part of a total farming labour force of over half a million people. It would be extraordinarily difficult for these people to change from 'chemical farming', as currently practised by most of them, to Fairlie's 'permaculture farming'. But as the inevitable crises develop, this may prove to be an essential contribution to the quality of life of all living here.[84]

Allotments and Vegetable Gardens

'Allotments are small parcels of land rented to individuals usually for the purpose of growing food crops.'[85] An average size is 250 square metres (a fortieth of a hectare). There are about 300,000 plots in the UK, mostly rented out by local authorities that are obliged to provide allotments where possible.

During World War II, food shortages led to many people developing allotments; by 1941 there were 1,400,000 plots – encouraged by the slogan 'Dig for Victory' and by books such as Alec Bristow's *How to Run an Allotment*, published in 1940, and described as follows:

> An instruction-book for the growing of vegetables which takes nothing for granted, and assumes no previous knowledge on the reader's part. Every detail is given about types of soil, the amount of seed required, the best tools and equipment to buy, when and how to plant, etc. etc.... The book carries a warm recommendation from the Secretary of the National Allotments Society [86]

Allotments and household vegetable gardens are more productive of food in terms of area than farms but, of course, more labour intensive, and so judged by economists to be less efficient! In terms of the satisfaction gained from seeing one's family eating home-grown food, they can be rated high in terms of their contribution to the quality of life.

Homesteads

While allotments could be available for many people, a change towards more homestead living could happen only slowly and over several generations, but with an appropriate educational programme, some people would see it as a satisfying way of life. It is instructive to examine the implications of living on a homestead as envisaged by John Seymour, in *The Complete Book of Self-Sufficiency* (1976):[87]*

> Myself, if I had an acre of good well-drained land, I would divide it in half and put half an acre down to grass on which I would graze a cow and perhaps a goat to milk during the short periods when the cow would be dry, a sow for breeding and a dozen chickens. . . . My remaining half-acre I would divide into four plots for intensive vegetable production, devoting a plot each to potatoes, pulses (peas and beans), brassica (cabbage family) and roots. I would divide the grass half-acre into four plots as well and rotate the whole holding every year. . . . I would have a greenhouse for tomatoes and hives for bees and I would plant a vegetable patch with extra household vegetables, herbs and soft fruit. (p. 20)

His insistence on having a cow is to ensure that the land is well manured and does not require chemical fertilisers. Seymour is a pioneer of convivial living. He says this by way of an introduction to his homestead life:

> Self-sufficiency does not mean 'going back' to the acceptance of a lower standard of living. On the contrary, it is the striving for a higher

* He has revised this as *The New Complete Book of Self Sufficiency: the classic guide for realists and dreamers* (2009).

> standard of living, for food which is fresh and organically grown and good, for the good life in pleasant surroundings, for the health of body and peace of mind which comes with hard varied work in the open air, and for the satisfaction that comes from doing difficult and intricate jobs well and successfully. (p. 7)

Certainly in the near future only a very small section of the population is likely to choose homestead living along these lines. Seymour's enthusiasm has to be moderated by the recognition that it is much harder for a family to aim for family self-sufficiency than for a nation to aim at national self-sufficiency. Seymour's way of life demands personal resilience and family coherence, as well as extensive knowledge of small-scale farming practice. But for those who can follow his lead successfully, as he says, life would be more joyful and thus in accord with the ethos of conviviality.

What Are the Major Changes Needed for National Self-sufficiency in Food?

(1) A dietary change in which less meat is eaten, but more grain. The argument is this: it takes about five times as much grain to feed an animal to turn it into meat as it does to provide the same sustenance to a human in the form of grain. Thus, an acre at present sowed with barley to provide animal feed could alternatively feed five times as many people if sown with wheat for bread. It is not necessary to become vegetarian: the change envisaged simply entails eating meat less frequently than is the case at present.

(2) A change in farming practice in which soil fertility is based on crop rotation and organic manures rather than on chemical fertilisers made with fossil fuel.

(3) A dietary change in which foods are available in the shops

during the local growing season, but not imported to extend that season. At present, for example, tomatoes are available in the shops all the year round: during the summer and early autumn they are home grown, but for the rest of the year they are imported from warmer countries further south, which entails both transport costs and the need to export something in return.

(4) A change in which more food is produced – in vegetable gardens and on allotments – by the people who will consume it. When food is grown on a small and local scale there can be sufficient helping hands to tend carefully the plants – by weeding, watering, feeding and protecting them from frost. It is possible to obtain higher yields per acre in domestic production than farmers can produce in mass production. The home freezer is an important part of the vegetable garden economy, enabling many fruits and vegetables to be eaten out of season, and the electricity to run it could come from solar panels.

(5) A change in waste disposal: food waste kept to a minimum and either fed to livestock or composted; sewage used as fertiliser.

(6) And much more – but, fundamentally, a political change which recognises that measures like these will safeguard the future.

10

Rethinking Money and Investment

If farming were to be organised like the stock market, a farmer would sell his farm in the morning when it was raining, only to buy it back in the afternoon when the sun came out.

—John Maynard Keynes (1930)

First Principles: how do people obtain money?

There are three *major* ways in which people obtain money: from work, from investment, and from gambling.* (Benefits, as a minor source of income have been discussed in Chapter 6.)

First, in order to feed, clothe, house and entertain themselves and their families, most adults work for money up to retirement age. In the past this was mainly the role of the males, while the females worked at home for no cash, looking after the children and maintaining the home. Today most adults, whether male or female, expect to work for money. The social tragedy is when, as discussed in Chapter 7, there is no work available and people need to rely on meagre benefits. A part of what people earn is paid to the government as a tax in order to provide public services available to all when needed, and to pay benefits to those unable for one reason or another to work. Many wage earners

* Gifts, benefits, inheritances and thefts are ignored in this account.

also pay a small part of what they earn into a pension fund to augment the state pension when they retire. Income from work, after tax deductions, is described here as 'take-home' wage.

Second, when people find, for one reason or another, that they have more money than they need for day-by-day living they usually invest it. This may be in the form of a bank or building society deposit, which pays interest; or it may be in the form of bonds, which pay interest and return the capital invested at the end of the maturity period, or in the form of stocks and shares in enterprises, which pay a dividend (provided the enterprise prospers). Income in this category is described here as 'interest-and-dividend' income.

Third, many people have a great desire to get rich quickly, and see the chance of a substantial gambling gain as the route to riches. Buying a national lottery ticket, having a flutter on the horses or on greyhound racing, playing for money in a game of cards, betting on the outcome of a wide range of social events that the bookmakers offer odds on – these are all activities seemingly hard-wired into the DNA of many people. Similarly, people at home with a little surplus money and spare time peruse the financial columns of their daily newspaper and, from time to time, contact their stockbroker to move small sums from one investment to another. For them it's a hobby and if they win a little, or lose a little, it doesn't affect anybody beyond their own family. Small-scale gambling like this provides its participants with hours of entertainment and, except where it gets out of hand and becomes addictive, destroying family finances, does no damage to the world at large. But large-scale gambling, in the stock exchanges of the world and in the take-overs and mergers of big business, is a different matter.

Where Take-Home Money Comes From in the Private and Public Sectors

In most cases it is possible to see the relationship between work and society, and where take-home wages comes from.

Private Sector

For example, in the so-called private sector, farmers grow food, builders build, factory workers make goods, lorry drivers transport, shopkeepers sell, insurance agents insure, printers print, and so on. Likewise, the employees of bus and train companies, enable people to move about, as do taxi drivers and airline staff. In this sector, essentially, both employers and employees take home money because the cash value of their output is greater than that of their input. Thus, farmers sell their crops for more than it cost to grow them, builders sell houses for more than it cost to build them, etc. The cash differential between input and output pays wages for the workers, buys the materials used, pays the overheads of the enterprise, such as the cost of buildings, equipment and insurance, and pays interest on money borrowed from banks and dividends to shareholders who have invested money in the enterprise.

Competition in the private sector tends to keep prices down: if, for example, one farmer tries to sell his crops at a much higher price than other farmers, the buyers will ignore him, and he will go bust. One of the many functions of government is to make and enforce regulations that, for example, prevent all of the farmers getting together and agreeing to sell their crops at a high price. This point is developed below.

Public Sector

The public sector is different. Most doctors, nurses, midwives, teachers, social workers, care workers, police officers, and other public servants obtain their take-home money from government finances, collected through taxation, which also pays for the overheads for hospitals, schools, police stations, etc. The government determines the level of their pay and tends to keep it at the minimum level that will ensure that there are sufficient people doing these jobs. There is an ongoing tension between the politics of the right and the left over the costs of the public sector. While the political left wants to ensure that there are sufficient public-sector workers, paid by the state, to provide for the public services that the left deems necessary, the political right seeks to privatise many of these and wants people to pay for more of their social and medical needs in accord with market forces.

As I have argued in Chapter 4, while the public sector tends to work to an ethos of conviviality, the private sector tends to work to an ethos of wealthism.

All of the workers described above in both the private and the public sector make tangible contributions to society. But there is another part of the private sector for which the truth of this statement is doubtful – the financial industries. But before examining this, it is helpful to discuss market forces.

Markets and Market Forces

Fairly obviously, a market is where buyers and sellers meet to exchange goods and services for money. Economists assume that both buyer and seller trade from self-interest – the buyer after the lowest price, and the seller after the highest. They argue that when a number of buyers and sellers interact, market forces produce optimum results for both. In general, if buyers demand more than sellers offer, the prices rise, and if sellers have more to supply than buyers want, the prices drop.

Markets Need Regulation to Work in the Best Interests of Everybody

A simple examination of the sale of bananas illustrates the need for regulation:

'A' starts selling bananas in a town where none were sold before. They become popular, and when the demand for them is greater than the amount he can sell, he is able to put the price up. In effect the bananas are rationed, but instead of everybody having an equal share, the 'rations' go to the rich, and the poor go without.

Then 'B' starts to sell bananas across the street. Competition has entered the high street. In order to attract customers, he sells at a lower price than 'A'. Thus, a market in bananas has been created. If 'A' is a wise trader he drops his price and for a while the prices move downwards to approach the lowest price that either trader can afford – which we will assume is the same for both.

This shows markets working in favour of the customers – the buyers of bananas. But suppose that 'A' and 'B' meet over a pint of beer and say to each other, 'Our competition is affecting our profits badly.' So they agree that next week they will raise their price – both to the same extent. They profit accordingly, and the customers find they are paying more.

This state of affairs continues until a third banana seller arrives in town, and charges less than the agreed price between 'A' and 'B'. Unless 'C' can be persuaded to join the cartel (as it is called) and falls in line with the price agreement of 'A' and 'B', market forces will operate again to bring the price down for customers.

Clearly it is in the interests of all the banana sellers to join the cartel. This is a way in which the market can work in favour of the traders – but not in the best interests of the customers.

Suppose the customers appeal to the civic authority to act. Because the civic authority is elected by all of the people, and there are many more customers than banana sellers, the authority will rule that the cartel is illegal and that, if the banana sellers are found to be fixing the price among themselves, they will be fined, or worse.

So now the price of bananas will vary and each trader will be trying to offer a lower price than his competitors in order to sell his goods.

This suggests that markets only work in the best interests of the customers if there are regulations which constrain the profit-seeking actions of the traders. So what were the consequences of the deregulation of the financial industries that took place in the 1980s? First we need a bird's-eye view of these industries.

The Financial Industries

We saw above how, in the cases of most private- and public-sector jobs, people earn their take-home pay. But what do people in the financial part of the private sector do? Where does their take-home pay come from?

Take-Home Pay of Employees in the High Street Banks: the retail business

In terms of high street banks it is fairly clear where the take-home pay of the employees comes from. In today's world, most people have bank accounts. Their bank receives their wage or salary, pays on request their bills, provides them with cash for incidental purchases, lends them small sums (called an overdraft, for which the bank charges interest) if their account runs short of money, and pays them a small amount of interest if they have savings in it. These are the so-called retail functions of a bank, and they extend to lending local businesses money, if they judge them reliable, in order to maintain or develop their businesses. In principle, in a retail bank, the take-home pay of the staff arises from the difference between the lower interest rate paid to those who lend money to the bank (i.e. the savers) and the higher interest rate of those who borrow that money from the bank. And, as elsewhere in the private sector, this differential also has to pay for the overheads of the bank.

But What of Other Parts of the Financial Industries?

The high street bank workers comprise only a small fraction of those employed in the financial industries. There are stockbrokers, market traders, investment bankers, hedge fund operators, and others of this ilk who make their money from their own gambling or from commissions from supporting the gambling of others. Young brokers frantically buy and sell shares in stock exchanges around the world, making and sometimes losing fortunes for other people, while computers, programmed with financial algorithms, make small gains or losses in seconds. So, how do the stock exchanges work?

Stock Exchanges[88]

A stock exchange is a place where stockbrokers and traders trade stocks and other financial instruments.* Stockbrokers buy and sell shares in stock at a stock exchange on behalf of clients, following their instructions. They get a commission on transactions. Traders work for an investment bank or similar

* This is a simple and basic account. In practice, the London Stock Exchange, for example, is a complex mass of different financial activities.

organisation and trade in stocks and other investments, making their own judgements in order to make a profit for the bank. If very successful, they attract high bonuses; if unsuccessful, they may be dismissed. Theirs are the 'high-octane' jobs.

The New York Stock Exchange (NYSE) is the largest in the world, the Tokyo Stock Exchange the second and the London Stock Exchange the third and oldest. Stock exchanges may be seen as 'legalised gambling dens'. In simple and naïve terms this is how the gambling happens.

The Big Bananas Company offers shares of stock at £1 each. Both 'C' and 'D' invest £100 and obtain 100 shares each. A few days later a newspaper article describes a new blight that kills off banana plants. Investors in Big Bananas take fright and start to sell their shares, and so the value of each share drops. 'C' watches the share price and sells all his 100 shares when the value drops to 90p: he gets £90 and holds on to it. 'D' is slower to realise what is happening, but suddenly sees that the share price has dropped to 40p, panics and sells: he gets £40 for his 100 shares. A later newspaper article says that a readily available fungicide can control the new blight easily. 'C' is still watching the share price and sees it start to climb. When it is 45p a share he spends his £90 and buys 200 shares. Within a month the share price has climbed to 80p. 'C' sells his 200 shares and gets £160 for them. Thus in the space of a few weeks 'C' has made £60 and 'D' lost the same amount. When the share price eventually climbs back to £1 per share, 'D' regrets that he sold when he did and 'C' regrets that he didn't wait longer to part with his shares!

So, stock exchanges are market places where people are buying and selling. Sometimes it is what the traders call a 'bull' market – when overall prices are rising – and other times a 'bear' market – when prices are falling. Every day of trading, the overall movement of prices is recorded in a variety of indices, of which the FTSE 100 is the best known.

The FTSE 100 ('footsie') is a weighted index of the share prices of the top 100 UK firms calculated every 15 seconds during stock exchange trading and based on the sum of the current share price of the 100 top companies multiplied by the companies' stock capital. It is seen as a measure of business prosperity, and features in daily media reports. It started at 1000 on 3 January 1984 and soared to nearly 7000 (at the end of December 1999), then dropped to below 3500 in March 2009.

Here is an example of a media report that shows some of the influences on market prices. It is part of the financial column of 11 November 2011 of Nick Fletcher of the *Guardian*; at this time, the finances of Europe were in turmoil.

> Overall the **FTSE 100** finished 15.56 points lower at 5444.82. As Greece finally chose a new prime minister and Italy moved closer to doing the same, there was a calmer air for much of the day, with Italian bond yields edging below the key 7% level. . . . **Experian** was the leading FTSE 100 riser, up 42p to 826p as the credit information specialist reported a 20% rise in first-half profits. A positive reaction to **Morrison's** results saw the supermarket group's shares add 11.3p to 317.8p. But **Admiral** fell another 67.5p to 820p in the wake of the car insurer's profit warning on Wednesday, which is based on increased personal injury claims. **Homeserve** recovered some ground after its recent plunge following mis-selling worries and fears of compensation claims. Its shares rose 37.5p to 256p after it said it had seen very few customers cancelling their policies. Social housing specialist **Mears** slumped 33p to 218.75p following a profits warning. The company said that in the wake of the government's decision to halve the photovoltaic feed-in tariff subsidy, it had decided to abandon its activities in this area immediately.

'The Big Bang' of Financial Deregulation

In October 1986, Margaret Thatcher's government, claiming that decline in London banking was due to over-regulation and the dominance of 'old-boy' networks, began to introduce changes, including computerised screen-based trading, an abolition of fixed commission charges, an abolition of the distinction between stockbrokers (who deal with investors) and stockjobbers (who hitherto had been a required link between stockbrokers and the market), and measures which enabled overseas companies to participate in stock exchange dealings.

The result was that deals that had previously been made face to face in the stock exchange could now be carried out in seconds by electronic transfers; also, it brought in US investment bankers who, frustrated by US law separating investment banking from retail banking, began to engage in investment gambling with the deposited funds of UK retail banks. In the words of Tony Greenham of the New Economics Foundation think tank:

> The Americans brought the idea that, instead of being client-based, it was a transaction-based business. You change from long-termism to short-termism, from looking after the long-term interests of your client to making the biggest buck out of today's deal.[89]

Heather Stewart and Simon Goodley, writing in the *Observer*[90] under the heading 'Big Bang's Shockwaves Left Us with Today's Big Bust', commented:

> Over the years, as investment banks developed increasingly sophisticated financial instruments, they became involved with one another in an ever-expanding web of bets and counter-bets, making them almost inextricably entwined.

They quote Professor Karel Williams of Manchester's Centre for Research on Socio-Cultural Change:

> Deregulation allowed the City to construct long lines of indebtedness, which are completely beyond technical regulation and, as we see with the eurozone crisis, beyond political management.

Investment Banking

Most of the high street banks, engaged in retail banking as described above, have investment divisions which, since deregulation, have been able to use the deposits in the retail side of the business – usually profitably.

One function of an investment bank is to provide financial advice and act on behalf of big corporations that may need to borrow money in the bond markets, merge with another company, or buy one up. This will bring appreciable fees into the bank. A second function involves the bank itself buying and selling major financial assets and speculating in the financial markets. Lawrence Knight of BBC News gave this example:[91]

> Suppose an investment bank knows a pension fund in London which wants to buy Russian mortgage debt, while its Moscow office may know a local home loans company. The bank may offer to buy the Russian client's loans, and then sell them on to the London client through a derivative contract, but at a much higher price. The profits on this kind of transactions are enormous at times when world economies are healthy.

These transactions are supposed to be risk-free for the investment banks – it is the buyer who should end up with all the risk. But as we know, to our cost, the investment banks' hidden risks have resulted in the government having to bail out some of them.

Government Intervention to Prevent Banks Going Broke

Northern Rock was a bank that provided mortgages to house buyers using funds raised by the bank in the money markets and that then sold these mortgages on to other companies. In August 2007 it could no longer sell these mortgages and hence was unable to repay its loans from the money markets. It had gambled, misjudged the market, and lost. In September 2007 the government gave financial support to the bank, but when the news of this became public it led to individual depositors, fearing that the bank might collapse and they would lose their savings, withdrawing their money as fast as they could – the first 'run' on a UK bank in 150 years. The government had to lend the bank £27 billion in a hurry.

That was the beginning. Then the Royal Bank of Scotland (RBS), one of the biggest banks in the world, had to be bailed out in 2008. Alistair Darling, Chancellor of the Exchequer at the time, tells the story in his autobiography.[92] On Tuesday, 7 October 2008, he left Downing Street before dawn for a meeting in Luxembourg about the insurance industry – in a chartered small plane to try to avoid press coverage, which might have exacerbated the existing banking crisis that involved the collapse of Icelandic banks supported by RBS. During the meeting he received messages that the share price of RBS had collapsed and that dealings in the shares had been suspended.

> When dealings in bank shares are suspended it is all over. I knew the bank was finished, in the most spectacular way possible. The game was up. If the markets could give up on RBS, one of the largest banks in the world, all bets on Britain's and the world's financial system were off. . . .
>
> I came out [of the meeting – where I was trying to look calm] to take a call from the RBS chairman, Tom McKillop. He sounded shell-shocked. I asked him how long the bank could keep going. His answer was chilling: 'A couple of hours, maybe.' I put the phone down and told my officials. 'It's going bust this afternoon.' I felt a deep chill in my stomach. If we didn't act immediately, the bank's doors would close, cash machines would be switched off, cheques would not be honoured, people would not be paid. . . . I rang Nick Macpherson at the Treasury and told him to tell Mervyn King (governor of the Bank of England) to put as much money into RBS as was necessary to keep it afloat that day. . . . There was no

> alternative but to keep the bank going and then to do what was needed to stop the firestorm. (pp. 153–154)

Lloyds Bank and HBOS, about to merge, also needed support, which was given by the government buying 43% of their shares. In 2009 it was clear that this merger was disastrous, since HBOS had bad debts owing to it, and again the government saved the bank from collapsing by increasing its stake in Lloyds to 65%.

By end of March 2011 the loans to failing banks and share purchases by the British government totalled £124 billion. Our government has had to borrow the money for the bailouts and, of course, is now paying interest on the loans – which it seems is higher than the interest being paid to the government by the banks. But even worse is the fact that the government bought 90 billion Royal Bank of Scotland shares at 50p a share and by September 2011, because of contraction of the stock markets, they were worth only 21p. Likewise, 28 billion Lloyds TSB shares were bought at 74p and fell in value to 31p. The National Audit Office, the source of these figures, said in a report[93] in December 2009:

> If the support measures had not been put in place, the scale of the economic and social costs if one or more major UK banks had collapsed is difficult to envision. The support provided to the banks was therefore justified, but the final cost to the taxpayer of the support will not be known for a number of years. The Treasury estimated in April 2009 that there may be a loss of between £20 billion and £50 billion, the wide range reflecting the inevitable uncertainty involved in such an estimate. The major determinant will be the prices obtained for the taxpayers' current holdings in the various banks.

What seems utterly incredible is that the senior staff of these banks were still taking huge salaries and bonuses. The *Financial Times*[94] reckoned that in 2010, 200 people working at RBS earned more than £1 million and at Lloyds 9 people received more than

£3.4 million, and it seemed that there was nothing the government could do to prevent these payments.

On 27 January 2010 I had this letter published in the *Guardian*; I'd written it because of a statement by Lord Myners (City Minister in Gordon Brown's government).

Yes, We Are Right To Be Angry

Lord Myners says 'We all need banks to take risks'. Sure – but what kinds of risk? What do we want of our banks?

We want them to receive our incomes, pay on our request our bills and keep us informed of these transactions. If we lend them money we want them to pay a fair rate of interest. We expect them in turn to lend that money to trustworthy businesses or individuals at higher interest – the difference being sufficient for the bank to pay its staff and maintain its services. We don't expect them to engage in casino-style gambling, and then come cap in hand when the bubble bursts.

What are banking services worth for watching over our money? Nurses watch over the sick, teachers watch over our young, social workers watch over the misfortunate, police watch over our safety. Comparable jobs merit comparable remuneration. Obscene rewards for playing the markets, advising on mergers that cost workers their jobs, and recklessly endangering the environment, are just causes for our anger. Investment banking may contribute to economic growth but little to the quality of life or the well-being of the nation. Yes, we are right to be angry.

Hedge Funds

Hedge funds are a particularly profitable and perhaps pernicious part of the financial trading. Wikipedia describes them as:

> … private, aggressively managed investment funds that utilize sophisticated strategies in both international and domestic markets designed to offset losses during a market downturn and/or generate returns higher than traditional stock and bond investments.

Recently they have begun to trade in food commodities, and this has had the alarming effect of pushing up global food prices. This is how the journalist Johann Hari described the recent world scene:[95]

> At the end of 2006, food prices across the world started to rise, suddenly and stratospherically. Within a year, the price of wheat had shot up by 80 percent, maize by 90 percent, and rice by 320 percent. In a global jolt of hunger, 200 million people – mostly children – couldn't afford to get food any more, and sank into malnutrition or starvation. There were riots in over 30 countries, and at least one government was violently overthrown. Then, in spring 2008, prices just as mysteriously fell back to their previous level. . . .
>
> The world's wealthiest speculators set up a casino where the chips were the stomachs of hundreds of millions of innocent people. They gambled on increasing starvation, and won.

A United Nations report on this issue, in June 2011, notes that the conversion of land use for crops for food to crops for biofuel production, changing dietary habits in urban areas, and adverse effects of climate change have negatively affected the supply of agricultural commodities. Nevertheless, it sees the 'financialisation of commodity markets' since 2004 as a major factor in price fluctuation. In less dramatic prose than Hari, it gives the same awful message:

> This phenomenon is a serious concern, because the activities of financial participants tend to drive commodity prices away from levels justified by market fundamentals, with negative effects both on producers and consumers.[96]

While grain prices fell in 2008, the UN report shows that by mid-2011 they had steeply risen again. It seems that hedge-fund traders follow a herd instinct and in combination cause big swings in the market. The UN report calls for regulation to curb speculation on food prices.

Advice on Tax Avoidance

Another aspect of the financial industries concerns the companies that specialise in advising their clients on tax avoidance. Nicholas Shaxson, in his devastating account of the financial industries, *Treasure Islands*,[97] gives a telling example – again based on bananas:

> Consider the banana. Each bunch takes two routes into your fruit bowl. The first route involves a Honduran worker employed by a multinational who picks the bananas, which are packaged and shipped to Britain. The multi-national sells the fruit to a big supermarket chain, which sells it to you.
>
> The second route – the accountants' paper trail – is more round about. Accountants might, for example, advise the banana company to run its purchasing network from the Cayman Islands and run its financial services out of Luxembourg. The multinational might locate the company brand in Ireland, its shipping arm in the Isle of Man; its 'management expertise' in Jersey and its insurance subsidiary in Bermuda.
>
> Say the Luxembourg financing subsidiary now lends money to the Honduras subsidiary and charges interest at £20 million per year. The Honduran subsidiary deducts this sum from its local profits, cutting or wiping them out (and the tax bill). The Luxembourg's subsidiary's $29 million in extra income, however, is only taxed at Luxembourg's ultra-low haven rate. With a wave of the accountant's wand, a hefty tax bill has disappeared, and capital has shifted offshore. (p. 11)

Shaxson notes that the *Guardian* found that in 2006 the world's three biggest banana companies, Del Monte, Dole and Chiquita, did nearly $750 million worth of business in Britain but paid only $0.24 million in tax between them.

He also refers to a finding of Britain's National Audit Office in 2007 that a third of the country's biggest 700 businesses had paid no tax at all in the UK in the previous financial boom year.

Public Concerns about the Financial Industries

Shaxson speaks for most of us when he writes:

> The corporate world has lost its way, and nowhere is this more true than with the big accountancy firms ... [They], responding to their clients wishes to cut their tax bills, have become steeped in an inverted morality that holds tax, democracy and society to be bad; and tax havens, tax avoidance and secrecy to be good.... What looks 'efficient' for an individual or corporation looks inefficient when you look at the system as a whole. (p. 31)

Is this what the so-called investment bankers do? Gamble with no concern for the consequences for others? In any gamble there are winners and losers, but in terms of the global commodity markets, beyond the investors who are winners and losers are the people whose living may be destroyed, their sustenance put beyond their means.

We may justly ask what the contribution is to society of these high-flying gamblers. By all accounts, they make only meagre payments of taxes (which they seem to vehemently resent). When a Robin Hood tax* is proposed which would take a very small contribution from their transactions, they are up in arms.

Perhaps I am wrong, but it seems that some of the international activities of investment bankers, hedge-fund managers and others in global finance involve playing Pass the Parcel in a game where each pass increases the value of the parcel, thus making big profits for the players, until the music stops and suddenly the value of the parcel plummets (i.e. the bubble bursts – in terms of another children's pastime). The result of the recent drop was that our government paid substantial sums to bail the bankers out and is now cutting back on public services in order to

* This refers to the proposed Tobin Tax on financial transactions – supported by most European countries, but rejected in November 2011 by the British Prime Minister, David Cameron.

curtail the national debt that arose in part from preventing the banks from going broke.

Yes, as Nicholas Shaxson notes in his conclusion to *Treasure Islands*:

> The recent crisis has made clear that much financial services activity is actually harmful.[98]

Anger at the activities of the financial world is global, as this report by Esther Addley in the *Guardian* on 18 October 2011 shows:

> In Madrid, tens of thousands thronged the Puerta del Sol square shouting 'Hands up! This is a robbery!' In Santiago, 25,000 Chileans processed through the city, pausing outside the presidential palace to hurl insults at the country's billionaire president. In Frankfurt, more than 5,000 people amassed outside the European Central Bank, in scenes echoed in 50 towns and cities across Germany, from Berlin to Stuttgart. Sixty thousand people gathered in Barcelona, 100 in Manila, 200 in Kuala Lumpur, 1,000 in Tel Aviv, 4,000 in London.
>
> A month to the day after 1,000 people first processed to Wall St to express their outrage at corporate greed and social inequality, campaigners were yesterday reflecting on a weekend which has seen a relatively modest demonstration in New York swell into a truly global howl of protest.

The New York Wall Street Occupy campaign inspired similar protests in over 900 cities worldwide. As Wall Street occupier Paul Buchheit said:[99]

> From 1980 to 2006 the richest 1% of Americans tripled their after-tax percentage of our nation's total income while the bottom 99% have seen their share drop over 20%.

It is the basis of the following reverberating slogan:

We are the 99%
We are the 99%
We are the 99%
We are the 99%
We are the 99%

In the City of London, the heart of the financial industries of the UK, *Occupy London* established an encampment outside St Paul's Cathedral in October 2011 as an ongoing peaceful protest against economic inequality, social injustice and corporate greed.

Vickers Report on Banking

In recognition of the widespread concerns about 'casino' banking, the coalition government in June 2010 set up an Independent Commission on Banking, chaired by Sir John Vickers, charged to 'consider structural and related non-structural reforms to the UK banking sector to promote financial stability and competition'. The report in September 2011 recommended that the UK's high street banking businesses should be 'ring-fenced' from the 'casino' investment arms of banking. The implication is that this would mean if the investment side goes bust, the retail side of a bank will not suffer. To many people's dismay, the proposal is that the banks should have until 2019 to implement this change.[100]

Rethinking the World of Finance

'Rogue trader' is a description given to financial traders making unapproved financial transactions on behalf of their employer. Wikipedia lists twelve such individuals who, since 1995, have each cost their employers millions and in some cases billions in dollars, pounds or euros. Leeson, in 1995, cost Barings Bank a loss of

$1.3 billion – which caused the collapse of the bank. One in September 2011 led to this letter of mine in the *Guardian* on 19 September:

> Sometimes naïve questions should be asked. What is the social value of the frenetic buying and selling of shares in the world markets? Do we need to be told, in every news bulletin, of the rise and fall of the FTSE? We hear of the winnings and losses of the big-time gamblers, but what is the justification for these games with money? One person's profit is another's loss.
>
> The slave trade was once seen as a legitimate way to make fortunes, so was child labour. Both were abuses of other humans. Perhaps one day stock market trading will be seen in the same light. Last week's evidence of another 'rogue trader' suggests that these questions should be answered.

Dr David Kynaston is an eminent historian of financial matters. Writing a thoughtful article in the *Guardian* on 25 October 2011 (on the 25th anniversary of the Big Bang), he seeks a 'cultural Big Bang' for the City:

> Severe faultlines in our financial system continue to bear heavy responsibility for the debilitating economic conditions that have persisted since the banking dramas of 2007–8. Reform is needed as urgently now as it was then, but over recent years dismayingly little has been achieved… .
>
> Will we see a more responsible City forsaking destabilising trading and opportunistic financial engineering in favour of providing a genuine, scrupulous, good-value service? It would be crazy to want finance to abandon its international role, but a readjustment of emphasis is possible.

It led me to send this to the *Guardian*, though it was not published:

> Today's City is, sadly, linked to greed, gambling and an obsession with economic growth. Environmentalists realise that, with the planet warming and oil peaking, economic growth must soon end – which is something those in City offices do not understand, but many camping on the City pavements do.
>
> The 'cultural Big Bang' that is now needed is to curtail the risk-taking gambling of the financial world.
>
> Perhaps a legal requirement that stocks, shares and bonds once bought must be held for at least six months before any attempt to trade them would be effective in stabilizing trading.
>
> Perhaps a limit to the size that any enterprise may grow to would reduce the extent of financial engineering that so often costs jobs and endangers livelihoods.
>
> Such measures might turn the City into the 'scrupulous, good-value service' that Kynaston looks for: one which serves the whole nation, not just the denizens of the Square Mile.

So, I put forward several ideas:

(1) Separation of retail banking from investment banking as soon as possible. This would enable the high street banks to look after the affairs of their customers and borrowers without fear that they could be imperilled by large-scale gambling by other parts of the bank. The Vickers proposal to achieve less than the full effect of this by 2019 is too long a period to wait. What further crises may occur between now and then?

(2) A legal requirement that stocks, shares and bonds, once bought, must be held for at least six months before any attempt is made to trade them. No doubt this would be heavily resisted by the investment gamblers, but its intention would be to change the culture of the finance industries from trying to make money from the ups and downs of stock prices to relying on dividends and interest payments on capital invested in companies. It would encourage shareholders to take an interest in the work of companies rather than focusing on changes in the stock exchange quoted prices.

(3) A legal requirement that boards of directors' existing duty to shareholders (to maximise profits) should be extended to a similar and parallel duty to employees to protect their jobs. At least one employee should be a member of the company board in order to promote this latter duty. Mergers and takeovers of companies should be subject to sanction by government, and then should only take place if there will be very few redundancies of employees.

(4) A limit should be set to the size of companies, so that too much power is not vested in the fiefdom of boards of directors. That limit should be set by government and might vary from industry to industry.

(5) As described in Chapter 6, there should be a maximum take-home-pay level of perhaps ten times the minimum wage, and anything above that that is paid as salary, bonus, or share-holdings to any individual should be taxed 100%.

Yes, these ideas will be seen as utterly preposterous to many in the financial industries. But we should remember that at one time state education for all, universal suffrage for men, and then votes for women were all seen as ridiculous notions that would damage the nation.

11

Rethinking Democracy and the Role of the Media

> *Government of the people, by the people and for the people.*
>
> —Abraham Lincoln (1863)

What is Democracy?

Those immortal words of Abraham Lincoln at Gettysburg on 19 November 1863 did not use the actual word 'democracy', though that was what he was talking about.

Another great statesman, Winston Churchill, said in the House of Commons on 11 November 1947:

> No one pretends that democracy is perfect or all-wise. Indeed, it has been said that democracy is the worst form of Government except all those other forms that have been tried from time to time.

In any discussion of a major societal concept like democracy, I think it is imperative for debaters to define the meaning that they attach to the term. My starting point is that democracy ideally embodies four fundamental principles:

1. **The rule of law.** This means that the State is governed by laws made by those in authority, who can only curtail the natural freedom of citizens if the law so permits.*

* There are three divisions of 'those in authority': the legislature – who make the laws (e.g. the UK Parliament); the executive – who apply the laws (e.g. the UK government of ministers and civil servants); and the judiciary – who endeavour to ensure the laws are applied justly, and who punish those who transgress them (e.g. the UK judges and magistrates).

2. **The rule of majority**. In choosing those to be in authority, citizens cast their votes in a secret ballot (held at least once every five years), and those with the most votes are elected. Likewise, in any assembly of those in authority, decisions such as making laws are determined by the majority.*
3. **The rule of freedom**. Traditionally, these are the freedoms of speech, of association and of assembly: these enable citizens to freely express their concerns to those in authority and to help each other to decide who should be in authority.

These first three are hallowed principles which in this country have slowly developed from clause 39 of Magna Carta† of AD 1215, from the Bill of Rights‡ of 1689, and through the heroic endeavours of people like the Tolpuddle martyrs of 1834, the Chartists of the 1840s, and the suffrage movement, with the eventual enfranchisement of women at the same age as men, at age 21, in the Representation of the People Act 1928, changed in 1969 to age 18.

Since the Beveridge report of 1942, with its five 'Giant Evils' in society of 'squalor, ignorance, want, idleness and disease', and the subsequent development of the welfare state, a further

---

* Of course, in small bodies, such as cricket clubs or village meetings, it is possible for decisions to be taken by the whole membership, as in the 'direct democracies' of ancient Greece, but it is more usual for a committee to be elected to act on behalf of the members. The protesters camping outside St Paul's have been using 'whole meeting' democracy.

† 'No freemen shall be taken or imprisoned or disseised or exiled or in any way destroyed, nor will we go upon him nor send upon him, except by the lawful judgment of his peers or by the law of the land', as signed by King John, AD 1215. (Notes: at this time it only referred to freemen; 'disseised' means to dispossess someone of their land unlawfully).

‡ 'That the freedom of speech and debates or proceedings in Parliament ought not to be impeached or questioned in any court or place out of Parliament' (Note: it only applied in this Act of 1689 to members of Parliament.)

principle which we can describe as democratic has become clear. I will call it the rule of social justice.*

4. **The rule of social justice**. This is the expectation that the State will endeavour to ensure that all its citizens have a good quality of life, with none too poor, and none too rich at the expense of the poor, and that they in return will individually exercise the responsibility of being good citizens.

In the introduction to this book I set out my present view of the 'good quality of life', listing those to which I suggest people are entitled. They deserve being repeated here.

For the adult:

- Work opportunities that provide sufficient income for needs, are personally satisfying and not over-demanding of personal time;
- A comfortable home for self and any dependents;
- Good opportunities to obtain food and other essentials of domestic life;
- Social opportunities that enable one to relate to others and build friendships;
- Leisure and entertainment opportunities and time to enjoy them;
- Travel opportunities;
- Freedom from fear; enjoyment of peace and tranquillity;
- Democratic freedoms, including living under the rule of law and benefiting from electoral opportunities;

* In part this was enunciated in the Labour Party manifesto of 1945: 'The nation wants food, work and homes. It wants more than that – it wants good food in plenty, useful work for all, and comfortable, labour-saving homes that take full advantage of the resources of modern science and productive industry. It wants a high and rising standard of living, security for all against a rainy day, an educational system that will give every boy and girl a chance to develop the best that is in them.' Twelve million people voted for that – Labour was elected and began to create the welfare state.

- Medical provision in sickness and in health, and good care in old age;
- Lifelong learning opportunities.

In addition, if some of these are missing, or in short supply:

- The hope that things will soon improve.

For the child:

- Safe nurture by loving adults, who share with the child, as appropriate, their entitlements listed above;
- Education in good schools;
- Happy friendships; and
- Good opportunities for play.

So, what of 'the responsibility of being good citizens'? These are points that come to mind:

- Recognising and supporting these same entitlements for others;
- Paying taxes as a means of ensuring these entitlements for all;
- Obeying the laws of the land and thus avoiding criminal behaviour;
- Contributing to affairs of state by voting wisely in elections and referendums.

It is the last of these that I shall discuss later in this chapter. But first, some data.

Elections: the rule of majority?

In the UK's general election of 2010, on the electoral rolls for the UK were 45,597,461 people. Of these, 65.1% actually voted. Table 5 shows the results.[101]

Table 5. Results of the 2010 UK General Election

Party	*votes cast*	*% of total*	*no. of MPs*	*votes per MP*
Conservative	10,703,744	36.1%	306	34,980
Labour	8,606,518	29.0%	258	33,359
Liberal Democrat	6,836,198	23.0%	57	119,933
Other	3,537,487	11.9%	29	121,982
Total	*29,683,947*	*100%*	*650*	*45,668*

Research carried out by the House of Commons library compared, for every constituency, the estimated number of people aged over 18 with the number who are registered on the electoral roll; the conclusion was that a further 3.5 million potential voters were missing from the registers.

(The turnout was in fact higher at this election than in the two previous ones: 61.4% in 2005 and 59.4% in 2001; but it was 71.4% in 1997 when Labour came to power under Tony Blair. The highest recorded post-war turnout was 83.9% in 1950 in a hotly contested election won by Labour in which Clement Attlee remained as Prime Minister but was defeated a year later by the Conservatives led by Winston Churchill in an election with an 82.6% turnout. In each of the six elections of the 1950s and 1960s more than 75% of electors voted.)

A poll by Ipsos MORI examined the age profile of the 65% who voted in 2010 (female, 64%; male, 66%), as in Table 6.

Table 6. Age Profile of the 65% Who Voted in 2010

Age	*percentage voting*
18–24	44%
25–34	55%
35–44	66%
45–54	69%
55–64	73%
65+	76%

These are some of the curious and worrying features of our election system:

- The Liberal Democrats, and on average the smaller parties, had to gain three-and-a-half times as many votes as the Conservatives and Labour to gain an MP. (Which, of course, is why they hoped the referendum of 2010 would replace the first-past-the-post election system by the alternative vote. They were disappointed.)
- While only 65.1% of the people on the electoral rolls voted in 2010, in terms of the complete population of citizens of voting age, only 60.5% took part in the election. Since 1950 there has been a persistent decline in election turnout.
- Young people are much less likely to vote than older ones.
- While the Conservatives and Liberal Democrats formed the coalition government in 2010 with a majority of 59.1% of the votes cast, in terms of the total electorate they had the support of only 38.5% – because 15.9 million had not cast a vote. Or, putting it in terms of the estimated total adult population of the UK (49.1 million when the estimated non-registered of 3.5 million are included), the government had been elected by 35.7% of

> the adult population. Before we get excited that this implies that in 2010 there is not 'majority rule', it needs to be recognised that this is usually the case.

No doubt the battle for a better voting system will be fought again, but here I want to focus on the second and third points. Why is it that around 40% of our citizens do not vote to choose their government? Why is it that of these non-voters, more are young people?

Some of the Likely Reasons Why Around 40% of the Electorate Don't Vote

- 'I'm not interested in politics: it's boring.'
- 'I don't trust politicians: they are all out for themselves, not for us'
- 'I don't agree with the policies of any of the parties.'
- 'I don't know what the different parties' policies are.'
- 'Our constituency is a safe seat so it's a waste of effort to vote'
- 'I'm in such a rush I haven't time to go to the polling station.'
- 'I was on holiday and didn't arrange for a postal vote.'
- 'I forgot.'
- 'I didn't know there was an election.'

What the Political Parties Spend on General Elections[102]

Table 7 shows how much was spent by the three major political parties in the general elections of 2005 and 2010, and how many seats were won.

Table 7. Expenditure and Seats Won By Major Three Parties in 2005 and 2010 General Elections

	2010 general election	*2005 general election*
	seats won/expendit	*seats won/expendit*
Conservative	306/£16.7m	198/£17.9m
Labour	258/£8.0m	356/£17.9m
Liberal Democrat	57/£4.8m	62/£4.3m

It would be facile to suggest that Labour lost the 2010 election because it had only spent half of what the Conservatives spent and less than half of what both parties had spent in 2005. What is more interesting is to see what these enormous sums, amounting to £1.67p for every Conservative vote and 93p for every Labour vote, are spent on. This is shown in Table 8.

Table 8. Analysis of Expenditures in 2010 General Election

Category of expenditure	*Conservative*	*Labour*	*Lib-Dem*
Campaign brochures	£0.7m	£0.4m	£0.2
Advertising	£7.5m	£0.8m	£0.2
Unsolicited material*	£4.8m	£4.2m	£3.1
Manifesto	£0.2m	£0.3m	£0.05
Market research	£0.7m	£0.5m	n.a
Media	£0.4m	£0.2m	n.a
Transport	£0.9m	£0.3m	n.a
Rallies and events	£0.9m	£0.8m	n.a
Overheads	£0.5m	£0.6m	n.a
Total	*£16.7m*	*£8.0m*	*£4.8*

*'Unsolicited material' refers to the leaflets produced locally in support of local candidates.

How the Political Parties Raise the Money for Campaigns

There are strict regulations as to how much parties may spend, and the UK Electoral Commission keeps careful records of how much is spent and from where it is obtained. Election expenditure represents only a part of the outgoings of the political parties. Table 9 shows the donations received by the UK political parties in the twelve months between July 2009 and June 2010, and from where they came.[103]

Table 9. Political Party Income for July 2009 to June 2010

Party receipts		*Overall donations*	
Conservative	£45m	Individual donations:	£38m
Labour	£24m	Company donations:	£17m
Liberal Democrats	£8m	Trade union donations:	£13m
Others	£3m	Public funds and other:	£12m
Total	*£80m*	*Total:*	*£80m*

The Electoral Commission does not give details relating one column to the other, but it can be assumed that 'company donations' went primarily to the Conservatives and 'trade union donations' to Labour. The Electoral Commission allocates £2m of public funds shared between all parties with two or more MPs 'who have taken the oath of allegiance provided by the Parliamentary Oaths Act of 1866'.

Contributing to Affairs of State by Voting Wisely in Elections

I have blithely stated that one of the signs of the 'good citizen' involves contributing to affairs of state by voting wisely in elections and referendums. I see it as an essential part of the privilege of living in a democracy.

Fundamental to 'voting wisely' is having a general understanding of the political issues of the time. I don't mean a detailed grasp of matters – that is something for the politicians and their advisers. The 'good citizen' needs an awareness of what is important for the future of society, a sense of priorities of what actions are needed, and a view, essentially personal, of which political party will best achieve the ends which she or he thinks important. Wise voting entails being to some extent informed.

We are a long way from this. Many people vote tribally – 'My father and grandfather were working men who voted Labour and so do I' or 'Now that we own our own house we belong to the class that votes Conservative.' Some vote according to what their newspaper tells them to do. Some vote because they like the leader of a party – or dislike the other leaders. Some vote for the party which has come knocking on the door asking, 'Can we count on your vote?' or for the party which has pushed the most leaflets through the letter box. As we have seen, many don't bother to vote. And a few – I hope I am not too cynical in saying 'a few' – vote after reflecting on the rival policies of the contending parties.

The evidence of Chapter 2, concerning an end to cheap oil, and Chapter 3, regarding climate change, shows that these are vital issues for the future of our society and, although they dare not recognise the importance of Chapter 1 – about an end to economic growth – both the Conservative Party and the Labour Party devoted sections of their 2010 manifestos to energy and climate issues, as shown by the following extracts concerning global warming and national energy production:

> ***Conservative***
>
> A Conservative government will cut carbon emissions in line with our international commitments and rebuild our energy security. We will make it easier for people to go green, with incentives for people to do the right thing. We will promote small- and large-scale low

carbon energy production, including nuclear, wind, clean coal and biogas. We will safeguard our energy security by ensuring there is sufficient spare capacity in the energy system. The low carbon economy also provides exciting opportunities for British businesses. We will encourage private sector investment to put Britain at the forefront of the green technology revolution, creating jobs and new businesses across the country.

We need to generate 15 per cent of our energy from renewables by 2020. We can confirm our aim of reducing carbon emissions by 80 per cent by 2050 which entails clearing the way for new nuclear power stations and creating four carbon capture and storage equipped plants, taking coal and transforming it into a low carbon fuel of the future.

Labour

To avert the catastrophe of unchecked climate change we have begun the shift to a different kind of economic future. We will be on track for the transition to a low-carbon economy by aiming to achieve around 40 per cent low-carbon electricity by 2020. We are committed to meeting 15 per cent of our energy demand from renewables by 2020. We already have more offshore wind-power than any other country in the world, and our plans could see this increase up to 40 times, alongside other renewable technologies such as tidal and marine, solar and sustainable bio-energy. We have already decided on a new generation of nuclear power stations, and a programme of four clean coal plants with carbon capture and storage technology with a levy to fund them.

Concerning household energy consumption:

Conservative

We will make it easier to go green, including through a 'Green deal' to cut household energy bills. A Conservative government will create an 'electricity internet', based on a new smart grid that will interact with smart meters in people's homes, to manage supply and demand. We will create a 'green Deal', giving every home up to £6,500 worth of energy improvement measures – with more for hard-to-treat homes – paid for out of savings made on fuel bills over 25 years.

> ***Labour***
> We will make greener living easier and fairer through 'pay as you save' home energy insulation, energy-bill discounts for pensioners and requiring landlords to properly insulate rented homes. Through our requirement that energy companies provide subsidies for insulation, we will ensure that all household lofts and cavity walls are insulated, where practical, by 2015. By 2020 every home will have a smart meter to help control energy use and enable cheaper tariffs; and we will enable seven million homes to have a fuller 'eco-upgrade'.

But how many people read these proposals? Indeed how many electors actually had a copy of the manifestos? And, in a busy world, who has the time and energy to read the 120 pages of the Conservative manifesto (available online, or purchasable on paper for £5) and the 77 pages of the Labour one (available online)?

➢ *Suggestion for promoting wise and informed voting*

Suppose, however, that every elector across the country received a 12-page booklet, from the Electoral Commission, with a summary of what each of the three main parties would do if it formed the next government. The following passages are taken from the long manifestos of the Conservatives and Labour in 2010. I have reproduced them at length in order to show that they are substantial documents but ones that, sadly, few electors seem to get hold of. They demonstrate the complexity of today's politics and the enormous problem for anybody who, starting with no knowledge of current parties, would have in deciding for whom to vote.

Suppose, too, that anybody wanting to know more could find an elaboration of each item on the party website. So, someone concerned about climate change would turn to the Conservative website for items 9, 36 and 37 on their list and items 36 and 37 (what a coincidence) on the Labour website, and find the statements quoted above.

It might be appropriate for the Electoral Commission to restrict the number of 'election points' to be made to, say, 60 and to restrict the characters per point – Twitter-like – to 140. Certainly it would focus the minds of the authors of these manifestos – to the benefit of every reader.

Invitation to join the Government of Britain

(Extracts from Conservative manifesto 2010, slightly edited and points numbered)

1. Take action now to cut the deficit, stop labour's jobs tax, help keep mortgage rates low and get the economy moving.
2. Safeguard Britain's credit rating with a credible plan to eliminate the bulk of the structural deficit hanging over a Parliament.
3. Create the conditions for higher exports, business investment and saving as a share of gross domestic product (GDP).
4. Reduce youth unemployment and reduce the number of children in workless households as part of our strategy for tackling poverty and inequality.
5. Improve Britain's international rankings for tax competitiveness and business regulation.
6. Increase the private sector's share of the economy in all regions of the country, especially outside London and the Southeast.
7. Raise productivity growth in the public sector in order to deliver better schools and a better NHS.
8. Reform the regulation and structure of the banking system to ensure lower levels of leverage, less dependence on unstable wholesale funding, and greater availability of credit for small and medium-sized enterprises (SMEs).
9. Reduce UK greenhouse gas emissions and increase our share of global markets for low carbon technologies.
10. Use the state to help stimulate social action, help social enterprises deliver public services and train new community organisers to help achieve our ambition of every adult citizen being a member of an active neighbourhood group.

11. Direct funding to those groups that strengthen communities in deprived areas.
12. Introduce National Citizen Service, initially for 16-year-olds, to help bring our country together.
13. Back the NHS and increase health spending every year.
14. Give patients more choice and free health professionals from the tangle of politically motivated targets that get in the way of providing the best care.
15. Give patients better access to the treatments, services and information that improve and extend lives, boost the nation's health, and reform social care.
16. Improve standards for all pupils and close the attainment gap between the richest and poorest.
17. Enhance the prestige and quality of the teaching profession, and give heads and teachers tough new powers of discipline.
18. Restore rigour to the curriculum and exam system and give every parent access to a good school.
19. Take steps to reduce the causes of crime, like poverty and broken families. put the criminal justice system on the side of responsible citizens.
20. Take tougher measures against knife criminals and crack down on the binge-drinking that leads to violence.
21. Cut paperwork to get police out on the street and give people democratic control over local policing.
22. Introduce honesty in sentencing and pay voluntary and private providers to reduce re-offending.
23. Cut the cost of Parliament, cut the number of MPs and cut Ministers' pay.
24. Give citizens direct control over what goes on in Westminster, make government more accountable and safeguard the independence of the civil service.
25. Publish details of the money government spends and the people it employs.
26. Cut the unaccountable quango state and root out waste.
27. Put neighbourhoods in charge of planning the way their communities develop, with incentives in favour of sustainable development.
28. Make it easier for everyone to get onto the housing ladder.

29. Give individuals and local government much more power, allow communities to take control of vital services.
30. Give people the chance to have a powerful, elected mayor in England's largest cities.
31. Scale back Labour's database state and protect the privacy of the public's information; introduce a balanced approach to the retention of people's DNA, and
32. Reform the criminal records system so it protects children without destroying trust.
33. Support devolution and make it work for all countries, with a referendum on greater powers for the Welsh Assembly, and support for the devolved institutions in Northern Ireland.
34. Cut carbon emissions and rebuild our energy security with incentives for people to do the right thing.
35. Protect our precious habitats and natural resources, and promote a sustainable farming industry; fulfil our responsibility to hand on a richer and more sustainable natural environment to future generations.
36. Reduce carbon emissions in line with our international commitments.
37. Promote small- and large-scale low carbon energy production, including nuclear, wind, clean coal and biogas.
38. Safeguard our energy security by ensuring there is sufficient spare capacity in the energy system: include a 'Green deal' to cut household energy bills.
39. Protect and improve the UK's natural environment, and pioneer new schemes to improve conservation.
40. Push for reform of the Common Agricultural and Fisheries Policies to promote sustainable farming and fishing.
41. Promote high animal welfare standards.
42. Ensure that government procures locally produced food wherever possible.
43. Work towards a zero-waste society.
44. Defend our national security and support our brave armed forces in everything they do.
45. Work constructively with the EU, but not hand over any more areas of power and never join the euro.

46. Honour our aid commitments and make sure this money works for the poorest nations.
47. Create a National Security Council to oversee all aspects of our security, chaired by the Prime Minister.
48. Keep a commitment to succeeding in our mission in Afghanistan and ensure our forces have the resources they need to fulfil this goal; repair the military covenant with a series of measures to support service personnel, their families and veterans.
49. Engage positively with the world to deepen alliances and build new partnerships. Help reform international institutions, help those in need, and play our part in tackling climate change and the proliferation of military nuclear technology.
50. Be positive members of the European Union, but there should be no further extension of the EU's power over the UK without the British people's consent; ensure that by law no future government can hand over areas of power to the EU or join the euro without a referendum of the British people. Work to bring back key powers over legal rights, criminal justice and social and employment legislation to the UK.
51. Honour our commitment to spend 0.7 per cent of national income in aid, and ensure our aid is transparent and properly targeted: spend at least £500 million a year to tackle malaria.
52. Push for a trade deal which brings growth to the poorest countries, helps those countries adapt to climate change, and puts in place the building blocks of wealth creation.

A Future Fair For All

(Extract from Labour Party manifesto 2010: '50 steps')

1. Secure the recovery by supporting the economy now, and more than halve the deficit by 2014 through economic growth, fair taxes and cuts to lower priority spending.
2. Realise our stakes in publicly controlled banks to secure the best deal for the tax-payer, introduce a new global levy, and reform the rules for banking to ensure no repeat of past irresponsibility.
3. Create UK finance for growth, bringing £4 billion together to provide capital for growing businesses, investing in the growth sectors of the future.

4. Build a high-tech economy, supporting business and industry to create one million more skilled jobs and modernising our infrastructure with high-speed rail, a green investment bank and broadband access for all.
5. Encourage a culture of long-term commitment to sustainable company growth, requiring a super-majority of two-thirds of shareholders in corporate takeovers.
6. 200,000 jobs through the Future Jobs Fund, with a job or training place for young people who are out of work for six months, but benefits cut at ten months if they refuse a place; and anyone unemployed for more than two years guaranteed work, but no option of life on benefits.
7. A national minimum wage rising at least in line with average earnings, and a new £40-a-week Better Off in Work guarantee.
8. More advanced apprenticeships and skills accounts for workers to upgrade their skills.
9. No stamp duty for first-time buyers on all house purchases below £250,000 for two years, paid for by a five per cent rate on homes worth more than £1 million.
10. A People's Bank at the Post Office; a universal service obligation on banks to serve every community; a clampdown on interest rates for doorstep and payday loans.
11. Spending increased on frontline Sure Start, and free childcare, schools and 16–19 learning.
12. An expansion of free nursery places for two-year-olds and 15 hours a week of flexible free nursery education for three- and four-year-olds.
13. Every pupil leaving primary school secure in the basics, with a 3Rs guarantee of one-to-one and small-group tuition for every child falling behind; and in secondary school, every pupil with a personal tutor and a choice of good qualifications.
14. A choice of good schools in every area – and, where parents are not satisfied, the power to bring in new school leadership teams, through mergers and takeovers, with up to 1,000 secondary schools part of an accredited schools group by 2015.
15. Every young person guaranteed education or training until 18, with 75 per cent going on to higher education, or completing an

advanced apprenticeship or technician level training, by the age of 30.

16. Legally binding guarantees for patients, including the right to cancer test results within one week of referral, and a maximum 18 weeks' wait for treatment or the offer of going private.
17. Preventative healthcare through routine check-ups for the over-40s and a major expansion of diagnostic testing.
18. More personal care, with the right in law to choose from any provider who meets NHS standards of quality at NHS costs when booking a hospital appointment; one-to-one dedicated nursing for all cancer patients; and more care at home.
19. The right to choose a GP in your area open at evenings and weekends, with more services available on the high street, personal care plans and rights to individual budgets.
20. Access to psychological therapy for those who need it.
21. Provide the funding to maintain police numbers with neighbourhood police teams in every area, spending 80 per cent of their time on the beat visible in their neighbourhood; improve police performance through online report cards and ensure failing forces are taken over by the best.
22. Intervene earlier to prevent crime, with no-nonsense action to tackle the problems caused by 50,000 dysfunctional families.
23. Guarantee fast and effective action to deal with anti-social behaviour, including a right to legal injunctions for repeat victims, funded by the police or council who let them down.
24. Expand tough 'community payback' for criminals who don't go to prison, giving everyone the right to vote on the work they do.
25. Control immigration through our Australian-style points-based system, ensuring that as growth returns we see rising levels of employment and wages, not rising immigration, and requiring newcomers to earn citizenship and the entitlements it brings.
26. More help for parents to balance work and family life, with a 'father's month' of flexible paid leave.
27. A new Toddler Tax Credit of £4 a week from 2012 to give more support to all parents of young children – whether they want to stay at home or work.

28. The right to request flexible working for older workers, with an end to default retirement at 65, enabling more people to decide for themselves how long they choose to keep working.
29. A new National Care Service to ensure free care in the home for those with the greatest care needs and a cap on the costs of residential care so that everyone's homes and savings are protected from care charges after two years in a care home.
30. A re-established link between the Basic State Pension and earnings from 2012; help for ten million people to build up savings through new Personal Pension Accounts.
31. A golden decade of sport, with the 2012 Olympics as a great national and worldwide celebration.
32. Registered Supporters' Trusts enabled to buy stakes in their club, bringing mutualism to the heart of football.
33. Operational independence for major museums and galleries, with more lottery funding returning to the arts, sport and culture after 2012.
34. Protection for the post offices and pubs on which community life depends.
35. The BBC's independence upheld; and Britain equipped with a world-leading digital and broadband infrastructure.
36. Achieve around 40 per cent low-carbon electricity by 2020 and create 400,000 new green jobs by 2015.
37. Make greener living easier and fairer through 'pay as you save' home energy insulation, energy bill discounts for pensioners and requiring landlords to properly insulate rented homes.
38. Move towards a 'zero waste' Britain, banning recyclable and biodegradable materials from landfill.
39. Link together new protected areas of habitat; maintain the Green Belt; increase forest and woodland areas.
40. Ensure fairness for food producers through EU reform and a Supermarkets Ombudsman; and support post offices, shops and pubs in rural communities.
41. Referenda, held on the same day, for moving to the Alternative Vote for elections to the House of Commons and to a democratic and accountable Second Chamber.
42. Improved citizenship education for young people followed by a free vote in Parliament on reducing the voting age to 16.

43. Legislation to ensure Parliaments sit for a fixed term and an All Party Commission to chart a course to a Written Constitution.
44. A statutory register of lobbyists, with MPs banned from working for lobbying companies and required to seek approval for paid outside appointments.
45. Stronger local government, with increased local democratic scrutiny over all local public services.
46. Conduct a Strategic Defence Review to equip our armed forces for 21st-century challenges, and support our troops and veterans.
47. Use our international reach to build security and stability – combating terrorism and extremism, curbing proliferation, preventing and resolving conflict, and tackling climate change.
48. Lead the agenda for an outward-facing European Union that delivers jobs, prosperity and global influence.
49. Re-energise the drive to achieve the Millennium Development Goals, supporting sustainable growth and combating poverty.
50. Reform the UN, international financial institutions, the G8 and G20, and NATO to adapt to the new global challenges.

It is perhaps surprising that of the £29.5 million spent by the three main parties in the 2010 election, only half a million was spent on their manifestos. But £12.1 million was spent on the leaflets of local candidates:[104] glossy sheets pushed through letter boxes by party faithfuls that typically display a photo of the smiling candidate, and perhaps another of their family, a list of the 'good works' they have done recently, the committees they have sat on, and the vacuous statement that they stand for something like 'better schools, improved health services and a new car park in the town centre'. Local party officials know that distributing these leaflets is vital to getting people to vote, and the expense of putting out a second one a few days before the actual voting is well worth the effort in a marginal constituency; but this can hardly be seen as contributing to 'wise and informed voting'.

➢ *Suggestion for a more democratic funding of elections*

It is obvious from Table 9, above, showing political party income, that much of the Conservative money comes from the business world and much of the Labour money from the trade unions. Why do they pay? Obviously because they expect to get an advantage for their 'side' if their support helps the party that gains power. It is the old model of British industry, where bosses and workers are ever at loggerheads and vested interests struggle to dominate. It stinks. Call me naïve, but I want to see a government that tries to act for everybody – for one nation – for the quality of life of all.

It follows that instead of putting limits on how much any individual or organisation can donate to a political party, such donations should be banned. Elections should be funded solely from state funds, and it looks as though the £2 million that the Electoral Commission currently distributes to the political parties might be sufficient to fund the manifesto approach advocated above if the post office distributed the 12-page election booklets without charge.

Thus, I am suggesting that expenditure on elections should be drastically cut. Posters are unnecessary – banal slogans are an insult to the intelligence of voters. Local leaflets describing the virtues of candidates could be replaced by local newspaper features by journalists committed to non-biased writing, as well as by websites where local candidates run blogs and respond to questions; and, because the personal is important, candidates should wear out their shoe leather pounding the streets, knocking on doors and holding public meetings. Television debates should be funded by the television companies, and probably the current practice of party political broadcasts should be abandoned – they say so very little.

It may be that there needs to be an increase in state funding to give some support to the kinds of electioneering that I advocate, but the important point is that the present practice of parties needing to go cap in hand to the donor with implied policies supportive of them is anti-democratic, if not immoral.

Our Votes Create Executive, Opposition and Legislature

One of the important tenets of democracy is the tradition of the separation of powers* – between the *legislature*, which makes laws (the House of Commons – elected MPs, and the House of Lords – distinguished appointees: together constituting Parliament), the *executive*, which applies the laws (government ministers – chosen from MPs – and civil servants), and the *judiciary* (judges and magistrates), which endeavours to ensure the laws are applied justly and punishes those who transgress them.

It is clear, of course, that there is an overlap between the executive and the legislature in terms of those elected MPs who are government ministers: they apply the existing laws and also put proposals for new laws to Parliament.

This overlap happens because a general election serves at least three purposes: (1) it enables a government to be formed from the political party that has the most MPs arising from the election – with the duty to administer the affairs of the country; (2) it enables an opposition to be formed from the MPs belonging to other parties – with the expectation that it will challenge the government on such issues as it considers misguided; and (3) it creates a House of Commons (of all 650 MPs) which votes on new laws for the country, on the repeal of old ones, and on related matters on the basis of decisions made by the majority.

* Although this notion goes back in part to ancient Greece, its current formulation is due to the French philosopher Montesquieu (1689–1755).

But members of Parliament have another function beyond sitting in the House of Commons, speaking in debates and casting votes. In their constituencies they meet or correspond with people who bring concerns to them, and as MPs they try to resolve difficulties, either informally or sometimes by asking questions of members of the government. They attend local meetings, visit schools and businesses, and address meetings, and all of these activities give them insights into the political status of their constituency and so have a bearing on the views that they express in Parliament.

So for the elector there is a possible tension between voting for a set of *policies* for government to enact and voting for a *person* who will contribute to sober debate on new laws in Parliament, who may be invited to become a government minister if his or her party is in the majority, and at the same time who plays an active part in the constituency.

➢ *Suggestion for a double ballot: one for policies and one for the local MP*

During the abortive national discussion in 2010 on 'the alternative vote', Simon Jenkins, in the *Guardian*, suggested that ballot papers might have two sections: (a) a vote for the party (and party leader) for government; and (b) a vote for the constituency MP.[105] (Jenkins thought that the first vote should be based on first-past-the-post, and the constituency MP vote on some form of proportional representation. This issue will no doubt surface again.)

It would mean that in a general election every party vote would be seen as contributing to the formation of the next government, being either for or against the winning party. No one need think, 'It's not worth voting, because So-and-so always has a large majority and is bound to get in.' It would mean that voters could express their preference for a set of policies irrespective of the merits of local candidates – and, indeed, might sometimes vote for a local candidate who is not of the party they vote for in the party vote.

Yes, sometimes it could result in the government not having a majority of MPs but still having a majority of support across the country. No doubt it would lead to government caution, but this would enhance the ideal of the separation of powers between executive and legislature.

Influences on Government: lobbyists

Lobbyists are people employed to try to influence somebody else, usually governments, to support the interests of the lobbyists' employers. Big companies have much at stake when Parliament makes laws that may affect their profits, and so they employ people to try to influence ministers. This has been called 'power dispensed in corridors'.

At present there are few records of the extent of lobbying in the UK, although in 2012 the Liberal-Democrat side of our present coalition government intends to legislate for the registering of lobbyists and their interests. The possible scale of it can be judged from data on lobbying which are in the public domain about the United States and the European Union. It was recently reported[106] that around the headquarters of the European Commission in Brussels are 15,000 lobbyists, of whom 70% represent business interests and 10% environmental, human rights, and public health concerns. It is estimated that the annual corporate expenditure on lobbying in Brussels is between €750 million and €1 billion. In Washington DC, there are 17,000 lobbyists trying to influence the US Congress and federal legislators. The pharmaceutical industry spent over £1 million in 2004.

➢ ***Suggestions for a more open and therefore more democratic practice of lobbying***

It must be hoped that new legislation in the UK:

(1) puts into company law an audited requirement that company annual accounts clearly state how much funding has gone into think tanks and lobbying agencies;
(2) requires every parliamentary and government department lobbyist to be listed on a register that is public; and
(3) requires every academic paper into politically sensitive issues such as medical provision, defence policy, energy or climate change to carry a footnote indicating the source of any research funding supporting the work of the authors.*

Such measures would at least show the scale of the commercial and other interests which try to influence affairs of state. Contemporary politics covers so much ground, much of it complex, that it is valuable for those in power to be advised by those with appropriate knowledge. But if corporate interests are investing large sums in order to 'reach the ears of ministers', it looks as though the democratic freedom of speech is being subverted.

Power of the Whips in Parliament

There is a general expectation, in voting for parliamentary candidates, that if elected they will vote in parliamentary divisions according to the wishes of their electorate, or at least in terms of

* Perhaps I should state here that my research is funded by my teacher's pension!

their own knowledge and conscience. But as the Conservative MP for Totnes, newly elected in 2010, recently pointed out, this is not the case. Dr Sarah Wollaston, with 24 years' experience as a doctor, was told that, on the Health Bill, she must not speak or vote against the government. Several times she has spoken about the alien power of parliamentary discipline, as here:

> May we have a debate on the role and responsibilities of Parliamentary Private Secretaries? Is it appropriate in a modern democracy that Members of Parliament who are neither Ministers nor in the Cabinet should be forced to resign if they vote against the Government? Does not that restrict their ability to represent their constituents and disproportionately reduce the power of the House?[107]

Parliamentary discipline is maintained by the whips, who are described in the official website thus:

> Whips are MPs or Members of the Lords appointed by each party to maintain party discipline. Part of their role is to encourage members of their party to vote in the way that their party would like in important divisions.[108]

A recent e-petition[109] on this, from campaigner Steven Stewart, sought to abolish the whip system.

> Democracy is founded on the right for people to have a say in what goes on in Government. We, the people elect our officials on the basis that they will vote in favour or against a motion before Parliament that is representative of the views of their constituents and the general British public. Parliamentary whips are contrary to democracy by encouraging, pushing, poking, prodding, bullying and threatening our elected representatives to vote along the party line. This petition supports the abolition of Parliamentary whips, so that our elected MPs are free to vote in the way that represents the views of their constituents and the public, not the views of their leader.

It was not allowed on the grounds that this was a party matter and not one for government.

I have some sympathy for Stewart's view, except that I believe

MPs should vote in divisions according to their understanding and their conscience. It is not practical or even sensible to expect them to vote according to 'the views of their constituents'. Elections are a means of choosing someone whose espoused views are favoured by the electorate, but not a device for mandating their future actions. But if the whips were abolished, as Stewart suggests, or at least their power diminished so that MPs voted in their own right, it could make parliamentary debates more meaningful as a way of persuading members how to vote. Anyone who watches the proceedings of the House of Commons on television will be bemused by the frequent speeches made to a handful of members: the sad truth is that members do not need to be appraised of arguments for and against propositions – they are told how to vote by the whips!

However, I recognise that some of the issues that come before Parliament are so complex that only a few MPs will have a firm understanding of what is involved, in which case it is sensible that they follow the 'party line' or at least follow a colleague whom they judge to be well informed.

Rather than the solid phalanxes of votes of government supporters for and opposition members against particular bills, we can envisage a situation in which some on the government side of the House might vote against and some of the opposition vote for – without the threat of being disciplined by the whips with the punishment of being unlikely to be offered office. If the outcome is that some bills are lost, this should be seen as the manifestation of the wisdom of the House rather than read as evidence of the incompetence of the government.

➢ ***Suggestion for making Parliament more democratic***

Reduce the power of the whips by making some, if not all, parliamentary votes free from party control.

Influences on the Electorate: the media

I believe that one of the responsibilities of being good citizens in a democracy entails contributing to affairs of state by reflecting on the political issues of the day, as expressed by the parliamentary parties and by others, and voting wisely in elections.

Earlier in this chapter I have suggested that at election time the parties should produce substantial documents of intended policies which are made available to every elector throughout the country. But I recognise that these will be wasted if people are too ill-informed to recognise the importance of the issues put forward. This is why I believe the media has an enormous responsibility to educate us all in what is happening in the political sphere. While all papers give good coverage of sports events, criminal cases and celebrity culture, it is only the *Guardian*, the *Daily Telegraph*, the *Independent* and *The Times* of the daily newspapers that devote space to a discussion of political issues, while the *Sun*, the *Daily Mail*, the *Star* and the *Daily Express* give little space to such, and when they do, they tend to be didactic and tell their readers what to think. In Chapter 3 I have illustrated the banality of much press comment on the ecological issue of climate change. Television news broadcasts are much more balanced than most of the press.

On 26 September 2010, when the Murdoch scandal was beginning to surface, I had the following published letter in the *Observer* as one of several under the heading 'Focusing on Murdoch Ignores the Wider Media Responsibility':

> David Puttnam says that 'British Democracy is under threat if Rupert Murdoch wins control of Sky' (19 September). Wider than that the future quality of life of our children is under threat because of the failure of much of the media to focus on what is happening to society and its environment.

In a world which has dire challenges ahead the media should have a vital educative role. We are going to see enormous disruption, if not destruction, to the economic systems on which today's affluence depends. Climate change will lead to more humanitarian disasters and the consequences of global shortages of food, water and energy, in a world of increasing population, will lead to greater economic turmoil and more international strife. We must search relentlessly for democratic ways to establish peaceful and sustainable ways of living with a reasonable quality of life, today and tomorrow, for all across the planet.

We should expect our newspapers to find a way of balancing celebrity culture and sports news and comment with sufficient political, social, economic and ecological news and comment to enable the reading public to know what grave challenges face the world – and what parliament and government should be doing about them. At present most newspapers give scant attention to such debate.

As C.P. Scott said, 'a newspaper's primary office is the gathering of news'. News needs to be clearly separate from comment: confusing them has a disastrous impact on politicians whose decisions depend ultimately on how the public may vote at the next election. Condemnatory front-page banner headlines frighten politicians, trivialise debate and damage democracy.

Our government must find democratic ways of limiting the power of press moguls, perhaps by insisting on ownership being in the hands of trusts with publicly enunciated aims and requiring trust members to be resident citizens. Balanced political adult education should be one of those aims.

Freedom of the press is an essential part of what I have called 'the rule of freedom'. It must be the freedom for people to be informed of what is happening in our society and the freedom to debate serious issues, but with a freedom from excessive bias (either right wing, as with most of the press today, or left wing) and a freedom from the political predilections of its owners.

➢ *Suggestions for ensuring that the press is an agent of democracy*

When the next Commission on the Media is set up, part of its brief should be to find ways of ensuring that the aims and practices of every news outlet include a commitment to balanced adult education on the political issues of our time and the establishment of some kind of regulatory body that ensures that this happens. At a time of great uncertainty about how the future will unfold, but a time of certainty that global warming, oil peaking, and continuing economic chaos will have a major bearing on that future, it is vitally important that the general public, the electorate, are well informed on the issues on which they vote and which will influence their lives and the lives of future generations.

12

Rethinking Education for Future Survival

Above all, let us remember that the great purpose of education is to give us individual citizens capable of thinking for themselves.

—Labour Party manifesto (1945)

What is Education?

In *Education for the Inevitable,*[110] I describe education as being about worthwhile personal and social development, and about promoting worthwhile culture and worthwhile survival techniques, while recognising that different people at different times will have different ideas of what is worthwhile.

Education is experienced in many forms, and so my extended definition, expressed rather ponderously, is this:

First: education is the experience and nurture of personal and social development towards worthwhile living;

Second: education is the acquisition, creation, development, transmission, conservation, discovery, and renewal of worthwhile culture; and

Third: education is the acquisition, development, transmission, conservation, discovery, and renewal of skills for worthwhile survival.

This provides a basis for rethinking education.

Parental Worries

Every year, across England, about 600,000 rising five-year-olds start the schooling that will control much of their lives for the next thirteen years. Parents at first worry about their happiness, then about who their friends are, and, six years later, about test scores and which secondary school they will get to. Soon the worry is about the subjects that their children should choose. Then, when they reach eighteen the worry becomes whether they are going to try for a university place or seek employment – and whether they will be successful.

If the parents are also sensitive to the worries of others they will see teachers bedevilled by a government obsessed with standards, inspections, curriculum demands, pupil assessments, school league tables, and international tables of pupil performance. This frenetic activity is underpinned by a rhetoric of concern to create a future workforce that can compete in the international race for economic growth. Parents and government would do better to worry about whether this long period of formal learning will prepare their children effectively for the world they will inhabit as adults.

What Will Our Children's World Be Like?

What will this country, and the world, be like in 30 years' time, when these children are in the prime of life? In Part One there is an account of some of the knowledge we have of what is likely to be the case. We can hope that the economic chaos of the early 2010s will have been overcome and that economic growth is no longer the goal of richer countries like ours (Chapter 1). The supply of fossil-fuel oil will probably have peaked, the price having soared to make petrol and diesel transport extremely expensive if not obsolete, and as a result personal transport is more likely to be in the form of bicycles than cars, public transport will be essential for journeys to and from work, and the freighting of goods will be much more limited than today (Chapter 2). The world is likely to be hotter, with serious changes in climate and consequent problems with food supply, water availability and migrant populations seeking to survive (Chapter 3).

Current Schooling Geared to a Failing World

Undoubtedly for today's children the world of their adulthood will be different from ours. But the current school curriculum is geared to the failing world of today: business as usual; financial whizz-kids wanted; entrepreneurs needed to boost exports; obedient factory workers; clerical workers with high literacy and computer skills; the focus on an ethos of competition, a me-first culture and ruled by a feral elite.

Society should be worrying about what lies ahead for our children. We should demand a school education that will prepare them for the uncertainties of global warming, oil peaking, and economic chaos.

For their survival, young people need to develop physical fitness, cognitive skills, social sensitivities, civic skills, and environmental understanding. For their quality of life they deserve convivial values and cultural knowledge in many branches. As citizens they need empowerment to achieve a collaborative and sustainable way of life based on critical reflection about society. These are matters of lifelong learning which must begin firmly at school and be experienced joyfully. Too little of this is happening in our schools today.

Community Schools

An obvious consequence of the loss of travel opportunities will be that parents will want their children to go to the nearest school. Choice will be a quaint memory of the second Elizabethan age. The whole edifice of competition, choice and league tables will have disappeared. Estate agents will lose one of their 'selling points'. Faith schools will have to open their doors to all the local children and schools boasting a 'specialism' will find it an unnecessary burden. It will be important, of course, that every school is a good school, but since that goal is already the policy of government, we can hope that long before then it will have been achieved. Children will go to the same schools as all the other children in their community, and this will have important consequences for the development of communities.

Of course, there are those who predict that children will not need to travel to school but will attend virtual classrooms sitting at a computer in their own homes. It is an unlikely scenario. It is the blinkered view of those who see education as no more than the transmission of useful knowledge from teacher to student and who fail to understand that the social situation of discussion, argument, experiment and presenting a case is an essential part of learning.

Teachers Working Collegially

I hope that soon schools will be free from government controls and sanctions and will be run by their teachers, acting collegially in relation to the needs of the local community, and designing the curriculum accordingly, with no external assessments until diplomas at the end of students' school careers.

In collegial schools, teachers work as collaborating colleagues, sharing responsibility for determining the curriculum, the pedagogy, and the assessment of students.

Collegial schools will be very much more effective at providing every child with a worthwhile education than today's government-controlled schools which are dominated by fiat, inspection and testing. Likewise, they will be far more effective than those schools of the mid-twentieth century where each teacher was autonomous and the school lacked cohesion. Freed from government control, collegial schools will permit the professional commitment, experience and training of the teachers to flourish, while being accountable to the local community through the school governors for the effective education of their pupils.

End-of-Schooling Diplomas

There are far too many external assessments made in today's schools. These narrow the curriculum and detract from effective learning. Assessment is an important part of teaching, but until the end of schooling it should be done by teachers and communicated to students and their parents – but no further than that. League tables of school results should be abolished. Teachers must be trusted, as part of their professional ethic, to do their best for every pupil. The only external assessment should be end-of-school diplomas, as advocated by the Tomlinson Committee.

In 2004 the Tomlinson Committee reported* in these forthright and excellent terms:

> It is our view that the status quo is not an option. Nor do we believe further piecemeal changes are desirable. Too many young people

* In '14–19 Curriculum and Qualifications Reform' – report of a committee chaired by Mike Tomlinson and sadly rejected by the Labour government that commissioned it.

> leave education lacking basic and personal skills; our vocational provision is too fragmented; the burden of external assessment on learners, teachers and lecturers is too great; and our system is not providing the stretch and challenge needed, particularly for high attainers. The results are a low staying-on rate post-16; employers having to spend large sums of money to teach the 'basics'; HE struggling to differentiate between top performers; and young people's motivation and engagement with education reducing as they move through the system.
>
> Our report sets out a clear vision for a unified framework of 14–19 curriculum and qualifications. We want scholarship in subjects to be given room to flourish and we want high quality vocational provision to be available from age 14. These are different, but both, in their own terms, are vital to the future wellbeing of young people and hence our country. We want to bring back a passion for learning, and enable all learners to achieve as highly as possible and for their achievements to be recognised. We must ensure rigour and that all young people are equipped with the knowledge, skills and attributes needed for HE, employment and adult life.

I hope that secondary schools will be much smaller than today – perhaps no more than 600 pupils, so that there is a sense of intimacy and proximity to the local communities. Primary schools should not be more than a third of that size and could well be the focal point of the local community.

The Final Years of Schooling

If schooling continues to age 18, as is planned in current legislation, there should be special provision for the last two or three years. These young people should spend as much school time working in the local community as in the classroom or apprentice workshop.

They must be trusted to act as responsible citizens. Give them the parliamentary vote at 16.

The opportunities for teacher-led and student-led teams to engage in community work are tremendous: supporting elderly people, helping younger children in primary schools, growing vegetables, tending livestock, providing street theatre, enhancing local environments, erecting solar panels, planting trees, and through such team work learning democratic values and a convivial ethos based on harmony, cooperation, stewardship, self-sufficiency.

At the same time, good opportunities must be provided for the many who seek academic or vocational learning – while maintaining social coherence in the population of the school.

These ideas demonstrate the essential role that teachers will have in community development. As the late Professor Ted Wragg said:

> There is no higher calling. Without teachers, society would slide back into primitive squalor.

Endpiece

It's the ecology, stupid.

—Greenpeace (2009), parodying President Clinton's election slogan of 1992, 'It's the economy, stupid'

Austerity Ahead

There can be little doubt but that there are tough times ahead. Austerity is the inevitable agenda. Only those who live in the cloud-cuckoo land of denial about global warming and failure to recognise that fossil oil is a finite resource nearing its peak can think otherwise. But I realise that those of us who relate these two 'horsemen of the apocalypse' to the third – economic growth leading to economic chaos – are few in number. Hopefully Chapter 1 will be persuasive.

Let Us Hope that Lovelock is Wrong

James Lovelock, in his carefully argued and well documented book, *The Revenge of Gaia*,[111] published in 2006, says:

> Our future food and energy supplies can no longer be taken as secure from a world that is devastated by climate change. ... Once the Earth begins to move rapidly to its new hotter state, climate

> change will surely disrupt the political and trading world. Imports of food, fuels and raw materials will increasingly become inadequate as the suppliers in other regions are over-whelmed by droughts and floods. … The highly productive farmlands of eastern England will be among the first areas to be inundated. (p.17)

A year later he was telling journalists[112] he believes that within 40 years the earth's population will have been reduced by climate-change-induced floods, drought and famine from six billion people to one billion.

If the rich countries of the world continue to pursue economic growth – the business-as-usual scenario – he may be right. But there are two reasons why we can hope he will be wrong. First, the good sense of the industrial countries' governments may begin to curb the greed of their peoples; and second, even if the people's greed can't be restrained, as oil peaks and its unit price rockets up, its consumption will inevitably fall and so less greenhouse gas will be emitted. Whether oil will peak in time to avert disastrous deaths on the scale posited by Lovelock is uncertain. Clearly our governments should be striving for oil production to diminish: they should be preventing the oil companies from exploiting tar sands and from drilling in Arctic waters. Certainly the economic consequences of oil peaking will be serious, but nothing like the ecological consequences of it not peaking.

The Complexity of Rethinking

The seven chapters of this book on 'rethinking' show the complexity of our times and the wide range of issues that politicians should be tackling. It is alarming that our politicians rarely address these issues and that Parliament engages in very little debate relevant to them. Some of my suggestions will no doubt be judged as extreme – but for the sake of the next generation they at least deserve to be examined by the major political parties. I claim that they have coherence, that all fit within the ethos of conviviality, and that they have a firm relevance to the rest of this century by setting a framework within which the entitlements for everybody to a good quality of life, as set out in Chapter 11 and the Introduction, can be established and safeguarded.

The Issues are Worldwide

My arguments are mostly based on evidence from the UK, but they have a relevance to every other industrial country around the world. I believe that in the future, as the nations of the world mature, they will aim for self-sufficiency, trading in few commodities, engaging in cultural exchanges, providing low-energy opportunities for tourism (especially for their youth), sharing scientific discoveries, certainly avoiding military conflict, but supporting each other in times of crisis. We are a long way from that now.

Kill-joy?

There will be those who say that these are 'kill-joy' measures that will deprive people of their pleasures – their self-indulgent shopping therapy, their air flights to distant lands, their proud display of better vehicles than their neighbours', their over-mortgaged homes, their choice of expensive private schools, their expenditure on private health care and cosmetic surgery, their delight in designer-modelled clothes, their state-of-the art music systems, their electronic gadgets, their visits to expensive restaurants, their little-used boats in distant marinas, and so on. Yes, in a more equal society without economic growth, these pleasures will disappear. But these are extrinsic pleasures which can be replaced by simpler, cheaper and possibly more enduring intrinsic pleasures derived from living in local communities and engaging, with others, in cultural, recreational and sporting pursuits as well as working, paid or unpaid, at worthwhile jobs.

Message of Hope

Fundamentally I am an optimist. I believe we can establish a stable and worthwhile quality of life. But to achieve this, every adult, every child, has to work hard at it, for we have to learn to replace the greed of wealthism with the joy of conviviality.

Ending on a personal note, I draw on my experience as a child during World War II – a time of national crisis more threatening than any for nearly a thousand years, when the people stood firm, accepted rationing and many other restrictions on their freedom, and some gave their lives in what was seen by all as a struggle for survival. I tell it because we are on the verge of an ecological struggle for survival now.

> I was seven years old when World War II broke out: we lived in Orpington, a few miles south of London. My father was a local government officer working for Westminster City Council and travelled by train to London throughout the war. My mother was a housewife spending her time shopping, cooking, washing clothes, keeping the house tidy and walking me a mile to and from school in 1939. We didn't have a car. Father and I had bicycles. Mother walked. Longer distances were by train or bus. The railway station had a poster, 'Is Your Journey Really Necessary?'
>
> Father dug an air-raid shelter in the garden; a builder made it a strong brick-lined, concrete-covered shelter where we spent many nights during bombing raids. Father had been pacifist beforehand, but now joined the Home Guard, and regularly did fire-guard duty

overnight on top of Westminster City Hall. With my mother he fitted blackout over all the windows and then glued brown paper strips over the glass to reduce any damage from blast. When in 1944 a rocket landing nearby blew in some of the windows my mother simply swept up the broken glass and covered over the frames. Aged twelve I put on my scout's uniform and went to help neighbours board up their windows. We were fortunate to sustain no other damage and no injury throughout the war.

My mother joined the British Red Cross, learned first aid, gave blood at Orpington Hospital to wounded soldiers. Later she went to work at the Council Offices in the Fireguard Department – before marriage she'd been a short-hand typist and her skills were valuable. When father's shirts wore thin at collar and cuffs she reversed them with needle and thread: likewise worn sheets were cut and re-stitched 'sides to middle'. 'Make do and mend' was the slogan. She knitted socks and pullovers for us. Father repaired the soles of worn shoes with rubber patches.

They belonged to a local tennis club and when waste land at the club was apportioned for allotments they took one. Throughout the weekends of the summers of the 1940s they alternated between playing tennis and growing vegetables – potatoes, carrots, greens, marrows, beetroot, peas and beans. They had to learn how to double dig, sow seeds, nurture the plants, when to harvest, how to store, how to rotate the crops year by year. The slogan, of course, was 'Dig for Victory'. Mother kept garden fruit in Kilner jars, made jams, salted runner beans, preserved eggs with water-glass. When she went shopping she bought our allotted rations and used them carefully. Tea leaves in the pot were used more than once. I think our waste food – there wasn't much – was collected for pig food.

We had an open fire, burning coal, in the living room and another fireplace, rarely used, in the dining room: that, with the kitchen boiler and a movable electric 'radiator', were all the heating we had in the house. When it was cold we wore more clothes. The 'boiler' warmed the kitchen and provided hot water for kitchen and bathroom – one bath a week with a few inches of water. There was no central heating, no shower, no refrigerator, no freezer, no television, no washing machine. The cooker used gas. The wireless and the newspaper Father brought home were our sources of news. I listened to

> Children's Hour on the wireless and sometimes my parents listened to broadcast plays. They played solo or bridge with friends about once a week.
>
> I read a lot, played with Hornby trains, made Meccano models, climbed trees and made dens with friends, collected shrapnel from anti-aircraft shells, cycled to scout meetings once a week and went camping during school holidays. I walked to primary school (carrying lunch-time sandwiches and gas mask) and later went by train and bus to secondary school.
>
> Notwithstanding the peril from the skies and the austerity of our lifestyle we were a happy, contented family and, when the war ended, thankful to have survived while distressed for the families of those who lost loved ones in bombing at home or on battlefields abroad.

Thousands of families could tell similar stories. I tell it to illustrate the way in which, at a time of grave peril, families responded with resilience and courage and learned to cope with new ways of living.

I fear that soon the world will be thrown into another grave, but different, peril. I hope my grandchildren's generation will cope with new ways of living and find a quality of life in new ways, as my parents' generation did. But our generation has a responsibility to ensure that can happen by replacing today's wealthism with convivial policies which may ameliorate the inevitable hazards ahead of global warming, peak oil and economic chaos.

Data Sources

I think it appropriate to express my thanks to the many journalists and writers of the *Guardian* whom I have quoted and to acknowledge both the incredible search facilities of Google and the comprehensive knowledge base that Wikipedia provides. As these references show, I am also indebted to many eminent authors who have explored issues on which I have touched.

References and Notes

1. A friend, Roger Gale, lifelong resident of Burton Joyce and for many years chair of the Parish Council, unearthed this piece of local history. Also deserving of being named is Peter Quaintmere, the friend of my second story from Burton Joyce. Sadly neither has lived to see me recount these tales.
2. *Observer*, 15 January 2012.
3. *Guardian*, 7 January 2012.
4. US Bureau of Labor Statistics, http://www.bls.gov/
5. *A Blueprint for Survival*, E. Goldsmith, R. Allen, M. Allaby, J. Davoll and S. Lawrence (*The Ecologist*, 1972).
6. *The Limits to Growth*, D.H. Meadows, D.L. Meadows, J. Randers and W.W. Behrens (Club of Rome, 1972).
7. *Prosperity without Growth: the transition to a sustainable economy* (Sustainable Development Commission, 2009).
8. *Proceedings of the National Academy of Sciences of the USA*, 24 February 2009, 106 (8), 2483–2489.
9. *Philosophical Transactions of the Royal Society of London B*, February 2008, 363 (1491), 467–475.
10. http://blog.hmns.org/?tag+history–of-oil-industry (accessed 21 August 2011), Houston Museum of Natural Science.
11. 'Sustainable Management and the Built Environment', Foresight Report (Government Office for Science, 2008), p. 9.
12. Ibid., p. 196.
13. 'The Oil Crunch: a wake-up call for the UK economy', Taskforce on Peak Oil and Energy Security (ARUP, Scottish and Southern Energy, Solarcentury, Stagecoach and Virgin, February 2010), p. 4.
14. http://energybulletin.net/print/52311 (accessed 21 July 2011).
15. Ibid.

16. http://aie.org.au/StaticContent%5CImages%5CDECC_Report.pdf (accessed 19 September 2011).
17. Michael McCarthy, Environmental Editor, *Independent*, 6 September 2011.
18. 'Oil exploration Under Arctic Ice Could Cause "Uncontrollable" Natural Disaster', *Independent*, 6 September 2011.
19. *Guardian*, 14 October 2011.
20. Greenpeace campaign notes (28 November 2011).
21. http://www.chevron.com/deliveringenergy/biofuels/?gclid=CMfR8_SXqasCFZQOfAoduzfQ0g (accessed 19 September 2011).
22. http://www.ucsusa.org/assets/documents/global_warming/climatwe2030-app-g-biomass.pdf (accessed 19 September 2011).
23. Wikipedia, 'Algae Fuel' (accessed 28 November 2011).
24. Vision_2030_-_Roads_to_the_Future.pdf (accessed 28 November 2011).
25. http://en.wikipedia.org/wiki/Scientific_opinion_on_climate_change
26. www.aps.org/policy/statements/07_1.cfm (accessed 12 January 2012).
27. http://royalsociety.org/uploadedFiles/Royal_Society_Content/policy/publications/2010/4294972962.pdf
28. http://www.ipcc.ch/publications_and_data/ar4/wg1/en/spmsspm-understanding-and.html
29. M.T. Boykoff and J.M. Boykoff, 'Balance as Bias: global warming and the US prestige press', *Global Environmental Change*, 14 (2004), 125–136.
30. *Guardian*, 3 May 2008.
31. J.A. Krosnick and B. MacInnis, 'Frequent Viewers of Fox News are Less Likely to Accept Scientists' Views of Global Warming', Stanford University, December 2010.
32. *Tools for Conviviality*, Ivan Illich (Calder and Boyars, London, 1973).
33. *Small is Beautiful: a study of economics as if people mattered*, E.F. Schumacher (Blond and Briggs, London, 1973).
34. *The Social Psychology of Work*, Michael Argyle (Allen Lane, London, 1972). Citations from Pelican edition of 1974.
35. *All Consuming: how shopping got us into this mess and how we can find our way out*, Neal Lawson (Penguin, London, 2009).
36. *Zen and the Art of Motorcycle Maintenance: an inquiry into values*, Robert Pirsig (Bodley Head, London, Corgi edition, 1974).

37. *The Hidden Persuaders*, Vance Packard (Penguin, London, 1957).
38. *The Advertising Effect*, Zoe Gannon and Neal Lawson (Compass, London, 2010).
39. Grantland Rice in his poem 'Alumnus Football' in the *Nashville Tennessean* (1908)
40. Larry Elliott, *Guardian*, 7 October 2011.
41. David Lloyd George's 'Limehouse speech': http://www.liberalhistory.org.uk/item_single.php?item_id=47&item=history&print=1 (accessed 7 October 2011).
42. *The Spirit Level: why more equal societies almost always do better*, R. Wilkinson and K. Pickett (Allen Lane, London, 2009).
43. *A Blueprint for a Safer Planet*, Nicholas Stern (Bodley Head, London, 2009).
44. Robert Kennedy, http://www.mccombs.utexas.edu/faculty/michael.brandl/main%20page%20items/Kennedy%20on%20GNP.htm (accessed 7 October 2011).
45. *Why We Disagree about Climate Change: understanding controversy, inaction and opportunity*, M. Hulme (Cambridge University Press, Cambridge, 2009).
46. *The Age of Stupid*, directed by Franny Armstrong, 2009; http://www.notstupid.org (accessed 7 October 2011).
47. *The Storm: the world economic crisis and what it means*, Vince Cable (Atlantic Books, London, 2009).
48. *Resurgence*, 110 (1985), 12–13 May/June.
49. *Basic Income, Unemployment and Compensatory Justice*, L. Groot, L.F.M. Groot and P. van Parijs (Springer, Dordrecht, 2004).
50. http://www.citizensincome.org (accessed 7 October 2011).
51. http://www.citizensadvice.org.uk/press_office201022 (accessed 10 October 2011).
52. Joseph Rowntree Foundation *A Minimum Income Standard for Britain* (2008)
53. http://www.jrf.org.uk/publications/minimum-income-standard-britain-what-people-think; http://www.jrf.org.uk/publications/minimum-income-rural-households (accessed 10 October 2011).
54. http://www.citizensuk.org/campaigns/living-wage-campaign/ (accessed 10 October 2011).
55. http://highpaycommission.co.uk/wp-content/uploads/2011/11/HPC_final_report_WEB.pdf

56. *The Spirit Level*, Wilkinson and Pickett. (see ref. 42)
57. *Good News Bible*, Ecclesiastes, Chapter 3, verses 9–13.
58. *The Times*, 13 April 2009.
59. http://www.greenparty.org.uk/policies.html (accessed 12 October 2011).
60. http://www.tradingeconomics.com/united-kingdom/unemployment-rate (accessed 12 October 2011) and *A Century of Change: trends in UK statistics since 1900* (House of Commons Library, 1999).
61. http://www.shu.ac.uk/_assets/pdf/cresr-tackling-worklessness-Wales-report.pdf (accessed 12 October 2011).
62. *The British Worker*, F. Zweig (Pelican Books, London, 1952).
63. *The Prophet*, Kahlil Gibran (1883–1931), (Heinemann, London, 1926).
64. *Small is Beautiful*, Schumacher. (see ref. 33)
65. *The Transition Handbook: from oil dependency to local resilience*, Rob Hopkins (Green Books, Totnes, 2009).
66. http://www.decc.gov.uk/assets/decc/11/stats/publications/energy-consumption/2324-overall-energy-consumption-in-the-uk-since-1970.pdf; http://www.decc.gov.uk/assets/decc/11/stats/publications/dukes/2312-dukes-2011–full-document-excluding-cover-pages.pdf
67. 'Government Pledges to Cut Carbon Emissions by 80% by 2050', *Guardian*, 16 October 2008.
68. http://www.theccc.org.uk/pdf/7993-Climate%20Change-ExecSumm-WEB-BMK.pdf (accessed 16 October 2011).
69. http://www.theccc.org.uk/reports/3rd-progress-report (accessed 16 October 2011).
70. http://www.official-documents.gov.uk/document/other/978010850 8493/9780108508493.pdf (accessed 4 December 2011).
71. Autumn Forecast Statement by the Chancellor of the Exchequer, Rt Hon George Osborne MP (29 November 2011).
72. Wikipedia: Nuclear Power in the United Kingdom (accessed 4 December 2011).
73. http://www.official-documents.gov.uk/document/other/978010851 0779/9780108510779.pdf (accessed 13 January 2012).
74. http://corwm.decc.gov.uk/en/crwm/cms/about_us/about_us.aspx (accessed 4 December 2011).

75. http://corwm.decc.gov.uk/assets/corwm/post-nov%2007%20doc%20store/documents/consultations/2009/2500%20-%20corwm%20interim%20storage%20report%202nd%20full%20draft%20february%202009.pdf (accessed 4 December 2011).
76. Professor Julia King's John Collier Lecture to the Royal Society in 2010.
77. Damian Carrington's article in the *Guardian*, 30 September 2011.
78. http://www.politicsresources.net/area/uk/man/lab45.htm
79. DEFRA Food Statistics Pocketbook 2011: http://www.defra.gov.uk/statistics/files/defra-stats-foodfarm-food-pocketbook-2011.pdf and www.defra.gov.uk/statistics/files/defra-stats-foodfarm-food-familyfood-2009-110525.pdf (accessed 30 October 2011).
80. Ibid.
81. Ibid.
82. Calculated from data in WWF report by Murphy-Bokern at http://assets.wwf.org.uk/downloads/environmentalimpacts_ukfoodconsumption.pdf (accessed 31 October 2011).
83. Simon Fairlie, http://www.thelandmagazine.org.uk/articles/can-britain-feed-itself (accessed 31 October 2011).
84. http://www.ukagriculture.com/uk_farming.cfm (accessed 12 December 2011).
85. http://www.allotment.org.uk/articles/Allotment-History.php (accessed 13 December 2011)
86. *How to Run an Allotment*, A. Bristow (1940, republished by Beautiful Books, London, 2010).
87. *The Complete Book of Self-Sufficiency*, John Seymour (Faber and Faber, London, 1976).
88. http://en.wikipedia.org/wiki/London_Stock_Exchange (accessed 22 October 2011).
89. http://www.guardian.co.uk/business/2011/oct/09/big-bang-1986-city-deregulation-boom-bust/print (accessed 21 October 2011).
90. *Observer*, 9 October 2011.
91. BBC News Business (online), 7 September 2010: http://www.bbc.co.uk/news/business-11211776 (accessed 21 October 2011).
92. *Back from the Brink: 1,000 days at Number 11*, Alistair Darling (Atlantic Books, London, 2011).

93. 'Maintaining Stability across the United Kingdom's Banking System', National Audit Office, 4 December 2009, Summary, para 19.
94. *Financial Times*, 4 February 2011.
95. Johann Hari, 'How Goldman Sachs Gambled on Starving the World's Poor – and Won', *Global Realm*, 2 July 2010.
96. 'Price Formation in Financialized Commodity Markets: the role of information', United Nations, June 2011.
97. *Treasure Islands*, Nicholas Shaxson (Bodley Head, London, 2011).
98. Ibid., p. 260.
99. http://www.commondreams.org/view/2010/02/04-7
100. *Guardian*, 12 September 2011.
101. http://www.ukpolitical.info (accessed 12 October 2011): a brilliant website for political data.
102. Ibid., and http://www.electoralcommission.org.uk/_data/assets/pdf_file/0011/109388/2010-UKPGE-Campaign-expenditure-report.pdf (accessed 14 October 2011).
103. http://www.electoralcommission.org.uk/_data/assets/pdf_file/0011/109388/2010-UKPGE-Campaign-expenditure-report.pdf
104. For an amazing collection of election leaflets, see http://www.electionleaflets.org/leaflets/ (accessed 15 November 2011).
105. *Guardian*, 7 July 2010.
106. Under the Influence, Actionaid, http://www.actionaid.org.uk/_content/documents/under_the_influence_final.pdf (15 November 2011).
107. Dr Sarah Wollaston MP, *Hansard*, 27 October 2011, Column 501.
108. http://www.parliament.uk/site-information/glossary/whips/
109. http://epetitions.direct.gov.uk/petitions/20152
110. *Education for the Inevitable: schooling when the oil runs out*, M. Bassey (Book Guild, Brighton, 2011).
111. *The Revenge of Gaia*, James Lovelock (Allen Lane, London, 2006).
112. Stuart Jeffries in the *Guardian* on 15 March 2007 and Sarah Sands in the *Daily Mail* on 22 March 2008.

Index